THE

GARDENING
YEAR

THE
GARDENING
YEAR

LANCE HATTATT

Illustrations by
ELAINE FRANKS

This is a Parragon Book
This edition published in 2002

Parragon
Queen Street House
4 Queen Street
Bath BA1 1HE, UK

Produced for Parragon by
Robert Ditchfield Publishers

Hardback ISBN 0-75257-494-9
Paperback ISBN 0-75257-498-1

A copy of the British Library Cataloguing in Publication
Data is available from the Library.

Typeset by Action Typesetting Ltd, Gloucester
Colour origination by Colour Quest Graphic Services Ltd,
London E9
Printed and bound in China

ACKNOWLEDGEMENTS

Many of the photographs were taken in the author's garden, Arrow Cottage, Ledgemoor,
Weobley. The publishers would also like to thank the many people and organizations who
have allowed photographs to be taken for this book, including the following:

Mr and Mrs Terence Aggett; Barnsley House; Polly Bolton, Nordybank Nurseries, Clee
St Margaret; Bromsberrow Place Nurseries, Ledbury; Lindsay Bousfield, Acton
Beauchamp Roses, Worcester; Burford House, Tenbury Wells; Dr Lallie Cox,
Woodpeckers, Marlcliff, Bidford-on-Avon; Kim Davies, Lingen; Dinmore Manor; Richard
Edwards, Well Cottage, Blakemere; Haseley Court; The Hon Mrs Peter Healing, The
Priory, Kemerton; Hergest Croft, Kington; Hidcote Manor Garden (National Trust); Kim
Hurst, The Cottage Herbery, Boraston, Tenbury Wells; Mr and Mrs J James; Mrs David
Lewis, Ash Farm, Much Birch; Mrs M T Lloyd, Edenbridge House, Edenbridge; Mr and
Mrs Roger Norman; Mrs Richard Paice, Bourton House; The Picton Garden, Colwall;
Powis Castle (National Trust); Royal Botanic Gardens, Kew; RHS Garden, Wisley;
Sissinghurst Castle (National Trust); Stone House Cottage Gardens, Stone; Malley Terry;
Raymond Treasure, Stockton Bury Farm, Kimbolton; Wakehurst Place (National Trust);
Wyevale Garden Centre, Hereford; York Gate, Leeds.

The photograph of *Rosa* 'Royal William' on page 117 is reproduced by kind permission of
Mattocks Roses and the photograph on page 148 by kind permission of Dr Lallie Cox.

THE AIM of this book is to show the gardener how to make the most of his or her garden through the months of the year. There are of course many factors that can affect plants – climate, weather, soil and even a gardener's own timetable of planting and pruning. If allowance is made for such variables, this book will provide a helpful working schedule.

SYMBOLS

Where measurements are given, the first is the plant's height followed by its spread.

The following symbols are also used:

○ = thrives best or only in full sun

◑ = thrives best or only in part-shade

● = succeeds in full shade

E = evergreen

Where no sun symbol and no reference to sun or shade is made, it can be assumed that the plant tolerates sun or light shade.

Many plants are poisonous and it must be assumed that no part of a plant should be eaten unless it is known that it is edible.

CONTENTS

THE GARDENING YEAR

THERE IS something pleasantly reassuring about the unhurried, cyclical pattern of the gardening year. With the gradual unfolding of each season the gardener experiences a deep sense of the harmony and continuity of nature.

SPRING

Sowing of seed, whether of vegetables, herbs or annual flowers, begins in earnest as the soil warms under spring sunshine. At this time of the year weeds appear, apparently overnight, calling for vigilance and the regular wielding of hand fork or hoe; alternatively, mulching of beds or planting ground cover will help to maintain order. These are months for the division of perennials, for planning the pots and containers you will use in summer displays as well as routine tasks like staking, conditioning soil and lawn care. As flowering bulbs go over, dead heading will avoid untidiness. Where these have been established in grass, mowing should be delayed until foliage has completely died down.

Nurseries and garden centres hold their largest stocks in springtime. A visit will reward you with new and unusual plants to revitalize tired borders, to fill recently developed areas, or simply, to plug the gap between spring and summer.

SUMMER

Summer is synonymous with scent and colour. Fragrant lilies, garden pinks, old fashioned stocks, tobacco plants and violas perfume the air from daybreak until dusk. Roses, the queen of all the summer shrubs, compete with clematis, honeysuckles, lavenders and mock oranges to fill the garden with a wealth of beauty. As the season progresses so the pastel hues of early summer deepen. Pale pinks, lemon yellows, lavenders and blues are replaced with fiery red, orange and gold, violet and indigo.

Opposite: China Pink tulips under a crab apple.

The ornamental onion *Allium aflatunense*.

Autumn

Traditionally autumn prefaces the end of the year, anticipates the onset of winter. Not so in the garden where, amidst the obvious signs of decay, fresh life stirs and a period of feverish, but satisfying activity begins.

Whilst the spent stems of summer are cleared away and dying leaves are raked from under shrubs and hedges, the newly revealed earth waits, freshly forked, for life to recommence. Evergreen trees and shrubs moved into new positions now will put out fibrous roots before the year turns.

Delphiniums and *Rosa* 'Fantin-Latour'.

Bulbs, legacies of summer lists, set out in open ground will, within a few short months, bring vitality to sleeping borders. September, October, or even November in milder areas, are the months in which to plant out spring bedding into final positions. Winter-flowering pansies, wallflowers, polyanthus and forget-me-nots, all easily raised from seed, will provide a wealth of colour in the weeks to come.

Work in the kitchen garden begins apace. With the main harvest over, vegetable beds are laid bare. Digging and manuring

Autumnal dahlias and *Fuchsia magellanica* 'Alba'.

ensures the ground is in fine fettle for the new season's crops. Seed sowing gets under way with carrots, cauliflower and lettuce for winter salads. Hardwood cuttings of currants, figs and gooseberries, taken as soon as leaves fall, should readily root in holding beds before the soil cools down.

Hamamelis mollis, the fragrant Chinese witch hazel.

WINTER

This is a time to consider the reshaping of beds and borders, the improvement of planting schemes, the repositioning of dominant features, the effective siting of pots – in short, a critical appraisal of the whole garden.

With the onset of a new calendar year winter sunshine, still rationed, becomes a powerful, irresistible force. Outside, neglected ground can be satisfactorily cleared and dug, paths made or relaid, toolsheds tidied and exciting new projects undertaken. As the year advances routine pruning gets under way. Included at this time are fruit trees and bushes, late flowering shrubs, roses, and those clematis requiring to be hard pruned.

But the winter garden is not without interest and colour. Viburnums and hamamelis provide deliciously fragrant early blooms, skimmias and hollies are bright with berry, the stems of dogwoods and willows gleam in sunlight and the ground is carpeted with first flowers. Amongst these are sparkling cyclamen, winter aconites, snowdrops, stalwart crocus and lovely miniature iris. The year moves on, the days are warmer, spring is in the air.

JANUARY–FEBRUARY

EARLY BULBS push through the cold earth to lighten the dark days. Lovely dwarf iris, drifts of crocus, pale snowdrops with sword-like leaves, tiny daffodils, all are the welcome harbingers of approaching spring. Leaves, retained throughout the winter, are prominent now. Lustrous ivies, clinging to walls and trees, shiny hollies, glistening laurels, the dull copper of beech, each contributes form and pattern.

Crocus tommasinianus Ideal for the rock garden. ◑, 10cm/4in

Iris unguicularis Rhizomes of the Algerian iris require an open, sunny position. ○, E, 60 × 30cm/ 2 × 1ft

Bergenia purpurascens Bold leaves throughout the winter months. E, 30 × 45cm/1 × 1½ft

Cyclamen coum To thrive, tubers should be planted in autumn in reasonably well-drained soil enriched with leaf mould or good garden compost. 10 × 15cm/4 × 6in

Galanthus nivalis Divide snowdrops immediately after flowering. ◑, ●, 15 × 15cm/6 × 6in

Eranthis hyemalis Plant the tubers of winter aconites in autumn. ◑, 10 × 15cm/4 × 6in

Helleborus lividus For a sheltered position. E, ◑, 45 × 45cm/1½ × 1½ft

***Helleborus foetidus* 'Wester Flisk'** Brilliant red stems and grey-green leaves distinguish this form of hellebore from others. All hellebores enjoy an annual mulch of well rotted compost. E, ◑, 45 × 45cm/1½ × 1½ft

Iris reticulata
'Harmony' Plant in
autumn. ○, 10 × 15cm/
4 × 6in

Chionodoxa luciliae
Glory of the Snow
should increase by seed.
10cm/4in

Crocus Spring-
flowering crocuses
flourish in grass.
10cm/4in

Narcissus bulbocodium Miniature daffodils are robust little bulbs which,
planted deeply in well drained soil, will reappear year after year.
○, 15 × 20cm/6 × 8in

INDOOR GARDENS

For those fortunate enough to own a heated greenhouse or, better still, a conservatory, it is possible to have something of interest, even exotic, in flower virtually at all times. Shown here is the enticing passion flower, *Passiflora antioquiensis*, which can be maintained in bloom through the winter months.

Cymbidium Cymbidiums are epiphytic orchids. Several forms bloom in winter. E, 75cm/30in

WINTER BARK

Once bare of leaves interesting and attractive tree trunks come into their own. Plant such a tree as the centrepiece of a winter garden.

Prunus serrula Bark the colour of polished mahogany. 9 × 9m/ 30 × 30ft

Acer capillipes A snake bark maple suitable for smaller gardens. 9 × 9m/30 × 30ft

Pinus pinea (Stone pine) Wonderfully tactile, bark such as this demands attention. 10 × 10m/33 × 33ft

Acer griseum Another small tree with peeling bark. 8 × 6m/26 × 20ft

WINTER SHRUBS

Imagine the garden filled with deliciously scented flowers throughout the darkest winter months. Such pleasures are easily realized by growing some of the winter-flowering shrubs. Positioned close to an outside door, or along a much frequented path where the fragrant flowers can easily and often be appreciated, these shrubs will be a source of enjoyment for weeks on end. Others may be grown simply for the effect of foliage. Evergreens are valuable at all times of the year, never more so than in wintertime.

Euonymus fortunei **'Silver Queen'** has a wonderfully wintery appearance. For golden variegation grow the smaller *E. fortunei* 'Emerald 'n' Gold'. E, 1 × 1.5m/3 × 5ft

Structure, in the form of trees, shrubs, hedges, walls and fences, indeed anything which affords permanent body and substance in the garden, is vitally important if the whole is not to appear flat and lifeless out of season.

Hamamelis × intermedia **'Pallida'** Spidery flowers, heavily scented, bloom on bare branches of the Chinese witch hazel in the first weeks of the year. 5 × 6m/16 × 20ft

Sarcococca hookeriana var. *digyna* Edge a path with this Christmas box to enjoy the sweetness of its small white flowers all winter long. E, 1 × 1m/3 × 3ft

Ilex aquifolium '**Ferox Argentea**' This holly sparkles with its green leaves deeply edged in cream. E, 2.4 × 2.4m/8 × 8ft

Chimonanthus praecox Wintersweet has fragrant flowers. ○, 2.4 × 3m/8 × 10ft

Clematis cirrhosa An evergreen clematis producing small flowers. E, 2 × 1m/6 × 3ft

Hedera helix '**Goldheart**' Use ivies to clothe unsightly surfaces. E, 9m/30ft

Pieris japonica
'Mountain Fire' An
exciting shrub.
E, ◑, 3 × 3m/10 × 10ft

Erica carnea **'Myretoun
Ruby'** tolerates alkaline
soil. E, 30 × 45cm/
12 × 18in

Lonicera fragrantissima
Heavily perfumed
flowers in winter.
3 × 3m/10 × 10ft

Daphne odora Nothing can compare with the
sweet, delicate perfume of the daphnes.
E, 1.5 × 1.5m/5 × 5ft

Imaginative use has been made here of winter-flowering pansies.

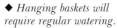
◆ *Hanging baskets will require regular watering.*

Outstandingly stylish, bay lends itself to clipping into shapes.

Young shrubs may be used most effectively in containers, as this window box demonstrates.

Light pruning from time to time will keep shrubs to size and in shape.

Compost should not be allowed to dry out.

Winter is no reason why
window boxes and containers
should not look as attractive
and colourful as in summer-
time. Here attention has been
given to form and texture to
create an interesting and
balanced display. Shaped box
balls contrast with the loose
form of the trailing ivies whilst
heathers, *Erica carnea*,
contribute a splash of warm
and welcome colour.

PRUNING CLEMATIS
Prune late-flowering
clematis. Reduce
growth to buds just
above the base.

Early-flowering clematis
require little pruning
but do it immediately
after flowering.

Clematis flowering
before midsummer
should for the most
part be lightly pruned.

PRUNING

Towards the very end of this period start pruning
the fully hardy shrubs that bloom in late summer
such as *Buddleja davidii*, *Hypericum calycinum* (Rose
of Sharon) and *Spiraea douglasii*. Leave less hardy
shrubs such as ceanothus, fuchsia, hydrangea until
any danger of severe frosts is past (see April, page
61).

Trees to be pruned, among them those grown for
the effect of their new foliage, include: *Acer
pensylvanicum* 'Erythrocladum', *A. negundo*
'Flamingo', *Ailanthus*, *Eucalyptus*, *Paulownia* (shown
above), *Platanus* (plane), *Populus* (poplar), and
Tilia (lime).

In the kitchen garden prune fruit trees and apply
a winter wash of tar oil. Similarly, spray peach
trees against peach leaf curl. Fruiting bushes
(blueberries, currants and gooseberries) should be
pruned and autumn-fruiting raspberries cut to the
ground.

IN THE POTTING SHED
A wet day is a good opportunity to sort through the potting shed. Use this time to service the lawn mower and oil and sharpen tools.

PLANNING THE YEAR
Freezing temperatures, biting winds, sleet and snow will deter even the most committed gardeners from venturing outside.

Now is the moment to plan changes and indulge new ideas. Ensure that the garden continues to evolve a distinctive and personal style.

CHECK LIST

- Flower indoor and tender plants in a warm conservatory (p.18).
- Grow trees and shrubs for winter effect and colour (pp.19, 20).
- Appraise the garden for form and structure (p.20).
- Plant window boxes and containers for seasonal colour (p.24).
- Carry out winter pruning (p.26).
- Apply winter wash and sprays to fruit trees (p.26).
- Check stakes and ties.
- Tidy and organize shed (p.27).
- Order supplies for the coming season (p.27).
- Plan changes and alterations to the garden (p.27).
- Plant summer-flowering bulbs (e.g. lilies) when the soil has warmed.
- Ensure you have taken precautions against cold weather (p.228).

PLANT DECIDUOUS TREES
Winter is the time to plant bare-rooted deciduous trees and shrubs if the ground is not frozen or too wet.

MARCH

SPRING BEGINS in earnest this month.
Newly planted trees and shrubs benefit from a top dressing of
organic matter to assist establishment. Hedges, purchased bare
root and planted in the autumn, should be checked. Firm any
loose soil and lightly fork in a sprinkling of fish, blood and bone
meal to promote growth.
In the vegetable garden there is still time to prepare the ground
before the major plantings of next month. Shallots, onion sets and
Jerusalem artichokes as well as garlic and early potatoes can all be
set out now. Potatoes will, of course, need protection from frost.

Tulipa kaufmanniana **'Gaiety'** Short stems and wide open flowers exposed to
the sun are a mark of the water lily tulips. Planted deeply they can become a
permanent feature. 15cm/6in

Narcissus **'Rip van Winkle'** Ideal for a rock or sink garden.
15 × 15cm/6 × 6in

Narcissus **'Thalia'** The ice white of 'Thalia' looks wonderfully startling against a dark background.
30cm/1ft

Narcissus **'Tête-à-Tête'** Low-growing daffodils withstand the wind.
20 × 15cm/8 × 6in

SPRING BULBS

To enjoy the effect of massed bulbs now, it must be remembered that they need to be ordered in summer for autumn planting. Groups of nine, eleven or more throughout a border will give both a full and natural impression.

Muscari neglectum Grape hyacinths rapidly colonize an area.
10–15cm/4–6in

Narcissus lobularis This small species daffodil is an excellent substitute for wild daffodils for it is low-growing and tough, perfectly capable of blooming through snow. 20cm/8in

THE WILD GARDEN

How evocative is the thought of a wild bank carpeted in moss through which grow tiny treasures of spring flowers. First would be aconites, followed by wild daffodils and wood anemones, cowslips and oxslips, celandines, clumps of primroses and, later, a haze of bluebells.

Scilla sibirica **'Spring Beauty'** Impossible to resist. This delightful little squill of intense delphinium-blue is erect in form and, because of its sterility, is long-lasting in flower. 15cm/6in

The inclusion of a few cultivated forms of plant will in no way detract from the overall picture.

Cardamine, the delicate lady's smock of meadow and ditches, hepatica, galium, the sweet woodruff flowering in partial shade, scented violets and soft-coloured primulas would not be out of place. Neither would the snakeshead fritillary *Fritillaria meleagris*, to flower a little later on.

EARLY SPRING PERENNIALS

Borders at this stage of the year still look somewhat bare as the summer perennials have yet to come into proper growth. It is, therefore, important to cultivate plants which, alongside spring bulbs, will flower early. Many of these early perennials have attractive foliage which will remain looking good.

Primula **'Dawn Ansell'** Double primulas enjoy rich soil. 15 × 15cm/ 6 × 6in

Corydalis solida Allow for partial shade as the year progresses. ◑, 30 × 30cm/1 × 1ft

Epimedium × *youngianum* **'Niveum'** Delicate flowers rise from fresh leaves. 25 × 30cm/10in × 1ft

Primula denticulata Drumstick primulas are easy to grow in any soil which does not dry out. 30 × 30cm/1 × 1ft

Anemone appenina Leave these lovely and easy rhizomes undisturbed to naturalize in a semi-shaded situation in well-enriched soil. 10 × 7.5cm/ 4 × 3in

SPRING DIVISIONS

The emergence of new basal leaves on later flowering perennials indicates a good time to divide.

Using a fork, lift plant and shake off excess soil. Divide into segments.

Discard the tired, woody centre retaining divisions of outer pieces. Replant with fresh compost.

***Ipheion uniflorum* 'Violaceum'** An absolutely charming front of border plant. 15 × 15cm/6 × 6in

***Ranunculus ficaria*
'Brazen Hussy'** For the
early spring. 5 × 20cm/
2 × 8in

Helleborus lividus
subsp. ***corsicus*** Flowers
begin in winter. ◑,
60 × 45cm/2ft × 18in

***Bergenia* 'Silberlicht'**
Spring flowers and
leaves all year.
30 × 50cm/12 × 20in

***Pulmonaria officinalis* 'Sissinghurst White'** The lungworts grow in clumps
and produce welcome flowers in blue, white or pink from late winter.
◑, 30 × 45cm/1 × 1½ft

Erythronium A genus that includes the pink dog's tooth violets, *E. dens-canis*.
They should be given moist, well drained soil in partial shade and left
undisturbed. ◑, 30 × 20cm/1ft × 8in

EARLY SPRING SHRUBS

Magnificent now is the large shrub or small tree, *Magnolia stellata*. This is one of the first magnolias to flower. For scent, the evergreen *Mahonia × media* 'Charity' is unrivalled, whilst the spectacular, near orange flowers of *Berberis darwinii* are bound to excite interest.

Forsythia Golden yellow flowers. Prune after flowering. 3 × 2m/ 10 × 6ft

Viburnum × burkwoodii Fragrant flowers, pink in bud opening to white. E, 2 × 2m/6 × 6ft

***Rhododendron* 'Praecox'** An early-flowering hybrid rhododendron. ◑, E, 1.2–2 × 1.2–2m/ 4–6 × 4–6ft

***Camellia* 'Water Lily'** Camellias require acid or neutral soil. ◑, E, 2 × 2m/6 × 6ft

LAWN CARE

A new lawn can be established at this time or in the autumn – see page 198 for details.

EARLY SPRING– lightly rake grass to remove debris
– first cut (set the blades high)
– establish edges with half-moon
– apply moss kill

SPRING – commence mowing and edging on a regular basis
– apply feed and weed

SUMMER – spot treat persistent weeds
– apply nitrogen feed

AUTUMN – scarify and spike compacted grass
– apply autumn feed
– final cut of grass
– keep off grass in frosty weather

MOWING STRIP
A lawn can be edged so that plants are able to spill over without impeding mowing.

REPOT PLANTS
Repot plants with fresh compost and a top dressing of grit.

CUT BACK ORNAMENTAL GRASSES
All of the ornamental grasses, like this *Stipa tenuissima*, remain attractive through the winter. Reduce to ground level in early spring.

PRUNING ROSES
HYBRID TEA ROSES Reduce all growth to 30cm/1ft above ground level. Remove diseased or damaged stems.
FLORIBUNDA ROSES As for Hybrid Teas but retain strong side shoots to around 15cm/6in.
SHRUB ROSES Cut away weak and damaged stems. Shorten other shoots by about one third.
CLIMBING ROSES Cut back side branches and tie in strong new shoots.
RAMBLER ROSES Any pruning should have been carried out immediately after flowering (see August, page 185).
MINIATURE/PATIO ROSES Cut out twiggy growth.

PRUNE FOR WINTER COLOUR
Salix alba vitellina 'Britzensis'. Pollarding has reduced growth.

The same shrub in winter, its warm orange colour reflected in water.

Many shrubs may be enjoyed throughout the winter months on account of their brightly coloured bark. Not least of these are the willows and dogwoods. Indeed, severe pollarding encourages strong, new growth.

CHECK LIST

- Top dress newly planted trees and shrubs (p.28).
- Plant shallots and onion sets. Sow early potatoes (p.28).
- Dead head early flowering bulbs (p.29).
- Plant a wild garden (pp. 30–31).
- Lift and divide summer flowering perennials (p.33).
- Plant new borders.
- Start programme of lawn care (p.37).
- Repot container plants (p.38).
- Cut back ornamental grasses (p.38).
- Prune roses (p.38).
- Pollard shrubs and trees grown for winter colour (p.39).
- Continue pruning fully hardy late-summer flowering shrubs (p.26).
- Under glass, start overwintered tubers of dahlias by watering and bringing them into the light.
- Protect new shoots from slugs, particularly herbaceous plants and clematis.

SOW HALF HARDY ANNUALS
Half hardy annuals should be sown under glass in seed trays or pans. As soon as seedlings break through, remove glass. Prick out when first leaves have formed. Harden off.

APRIL

APRIL MARKS THE START of a period of feverish activity in the garden. Winter wet is past and the drying winds of March make the ground, at least on the surface, dry, crumbly and workable. Bulbous plants provide much of the colour in the borders. Massed displays convey an appearance of fullness which is welcome at a time when many herbaceous perennials remain dormant. By carefully mixing daffodils and tulips, as well as other bulbs, it should be possible to have a continuous display for several weeks to come. Bulbs which have flowered earlier on should be dead headed and allowed to die down.

This charming mixture of pink hyacinths and white violas demonstrates the effect of mass planting. The success lies as much in the simplicity of the combination as in the number of plants.

Wallflowers (*Cheiranthus*) are one of the mainstays of all spring bedding.
Sow in late summer in readiness to be set out during the autumn.
30 × 30cm/1 × 1ft

Tulipa saxatilis Named the rock tulip, it is an
excellent choice for the rockery. 15cm/6in

Tulipa 'Apeldoorn' One
of the Darwin hybrid
tulips. 60 × 20cm/
2ft × 8in

Leucojum vernum The spring snowflake closely resembles the earlier flowering snowdrop. If left alone, in time *Leucojum* will increase, particularly when established in peaty soil which remains moist. 20 × 10cm/8 × 4in

To grow daffodils in this number in this way must, for many, remain a dream. However, pleasing results may easily be achieved by planting bold, generous clumps.

Fritillaria meleagris These snakeshead fritillaries do best when left to naturalize in grass as shown here providing that grass cutting is delayed until the flowers have had a chance to seed. 25cm/10in

Fritillaria imperialis Flowers, in red, orange or yellow. Bulbs are best planted on their sides on a bed of coarse sand or grit. After planting dress with sulphate of potash and apply each year at a rate of 25g/1oz per square metre/yard. 1.5m × 30cm/5 × 1ft

Enjoy these delightful, unassuming spring flowers in any semi-shaded situation. 15 × 15cm/6 × 6in

Primula **'Guinevere'**
One of many attractively coloured primulas.
15 × 15cm/6 × 6in

Lamium orvala Unlike so many of the lamiums which spread outwards to cover the ground, this one is clump forming. In the autumn look for self-sown seedlings. 60 × 30cm/2 × 1ft

Primula **'Hose-in-Hose'**
Flowers above a ruff of
leaves. 10 × 10cm/
4 × 4in

Primula **'Dusky Lady'**
The appeal lies in the
deep wine colour.
15 × 15cm/6 × 6in

Veronica peduncularis
'Georgia Blue' will carry
some blooms in each
month. E, 15 × 30m/
6in × 1ft

Arum creticum This showy species of arum makes
a spectacular spring display. 30 × 30cm/1 × 1ft

Uvularia grandiflora The bellwort is seldom seen in gardens. Peaty soil and some partial shade are all that is required. ◑, 30 × 30cm/1 × 1ft

Doronicum columnae The leopard's bane is an old-fashioned plant. 45 × 45cm/1½ × 1½ft

Brunnera macrophylla The Siberian bugloss bears forget-me-not flowers. ◑, 45 × 60cm/1½ × 2ft

THE WATER GARDEN IN SPRING

In many respects the pondside at this time of year is at its best. Always, of course, it is important to mask the edges of a pond. Plants which come into leaf early on are ideal for this purpose. For colour, look to the marsh marigolds, the skunk cabbages, the umbrella plant, *Darmera peltata*, cardamines, primulas, early saxifrages and ranunculus.

Lysichiton camtschatcensis A cousin of *L. americanus*, this has spathes that are white rather than yellow and appear slightly later. 75×60cm/$2\frac{1}{2} \times 2$ft

Caltha palustris The marsh marigold will flourish wherever the soil remains moist. ○, 30×40cm/ $1 \times 1\frac{1}{2}$ft

***Dicentra* 'Bacchanal'** Dicentras will succeed in any fertile garden soil. 45×30cm/$1\frac{1}{2} \times 1$ft

THE ROCK GARDEN IN SPRING

So many alpines are spring-flowering it is no surprise that the rock garden, traditional home of small plants which might otherwise become lost, should be full of colour and interest at this time of year.

The cultivation of these miniature perennials is not difficult. For most, the essential requirement is the provision of good drainage. This may be achieved by incorporating generous amounts of horticultural grit with the compost into the planting hole. A sleeve of grit spread around the neck of the plant will further assist drainage as well as creating a trim appearance.

Of course the rock garden does not have to be limited to flowering alpines. Tiny ferns, dwarf, slow growing conifers, diminutive bulbs, even small-scale deciduous trees are all worthy of a place.

Arabis caucasica
Intense white flowers. Its trailing habit is useful for tumbling over low walls.
15 × 30cm/6in × 1ft

***Tulipa* 'Purissima'** The milky white flowers of 'Purissima' are a sport of the well known 'Madame Lefeber', the red of which is quite different from any similar shade in tulips.
40 × 20cm/16 × 8in

Pulsatilla vulgaris Flowering at Easter, the Pasque flower is richly coloured deep purple with a harvest yellow eye. 30 × 30cm/1 × 1ft

Aubrieta deltoidea
Everyone is familiar with this spring carpeter for its loves to scramble over rocks, overrun inclines and creep into nooks and crannies. ○, 5 × 45cm/2in × 1½ft

Alyssum saxatile will flourish in drought conditions, indeed preferring a dry spot in infertile soil.
○, 15 × 30cm/6in × 1ft

Sanguinaria canadensis **'Plena'** Flowers of the purest of whites.
◑, 10cm/4in

Euphorbia myrsinites A ground-hugging spurge with whorls of lime flowers at the tips. ○, E, 15 × 60cm/6in × 2ft

Dicentra **'Spring Morning'** This is one of the loveliest of dicentras, enjoying a lengthy flowering period. 45 × 45cm/ 1½ × 1½ft

Viola labradorica An enchanting little viola. Allow it to seed through the border. 10 × 30cm

Anemone nemorosa **'Robinsoniana'** will naturalize where the soil is humus-rich. ☽, 15 × 30cm/6in × 1ft

SPRING SHRUBS AND TREES

Many of the evergreen shrubs flower from now onwards. Among these are camellias, whose glossy leaves are a perfect foil to waxy blooms, some viburnums, early rhododendrons and sweetly scented osmanthus. Flowering trees include a large number of prunus, noble magnolias, and willows with their fascinating catkins. Trees like *Prunus subhirtella* 'Autumnalis' are now a sheet of lovely, semi-double white flowers. Use the area at the base of these early trees and shrubs to grow small, spring bulbs. Some of the deliciously fragrant jonquil narcissi, such as 'Baby Moon' or 'Suzy', *Fritillaria michailovskyi*, or the powder puff heads of the feather hyacinth, *Muscari plumosum*, would all be suitable.

Salix lanata This dwarf tree is a worthy subject for the rock garden providing, as with all willows, the soil is not allowed to dry out.
1 × 1m/3 × 3ft

Acer pseudoplatanus
'Brilliantissimum' This small tree
in new leaf is quite spectacular, a
dazzling addition to any garden.
6 × 7m/20 × 23ft

Chaenomeles speciosa **'Nivalis'** This white
form of japonica is but one of many
varieties, red being more common. Of the
named reds, *C. × superba* 'Knap Hill
Scarlet' and 'Rowallane' are possibly
most widely grown. 2.4 × 5m/8 × 16ft

Camellia **'Nobilissima'** will benefit from leaf mould. ◑, E, 3 × 2m/ 10 × 6ft

Camellia **'Galaxie'** Those who garden on chalk will have to grow camellias in pots or tubs. ◑, E, 2 × 2m/6 × 6ft

Magnolia × *loebneri* **'Leonard Messel'** Spring flowering magnolias are surely one of the joys of this time of year. 'Leonard Messel' flowers on bare wood with lilac-pink blooms, deeper in bud. ◯, 8 × 6m/26 × 20ft

Magnolia × *soulangeana* This form, 'Burgundy', will, as others of the type, flower whilst young.

Viburnum × *juddii* This viburnum beautifully scented flowers. 1.5 × 1.5/5 × 5ft

Prunus **'Pink Shell'** An ornamental cherry with soft pink blossom. 9 × 8m/30 × 26ft

Rhododendron **Hybrid 'Lem's Cameo'** Hybrid rhododendrons are generally characterized by plentiful foliage, firm flower trusses and total hardiness. E, 2 × 2m/6 × 6ft

Salix caprea **'Kilmarnock'** The Kilmarnock willow is compact in growth and makes an excellent specimen tree. 2 × 2m/6 × 6ft

PLANT PURCHASING

A visit to a garden centre or nursery at this time of year will reveal an often bewildering array of trees, shrubs, herbaceous perennials, alpines and vegetable seedlings. The majority of these will be offered for sale in pots as container-grown. This is a convenient and reliable way of buying plants.

See page 27 for planting bare-root.

Berberis darwinii
Flower in spring, berries in autumn.
E, 4 × 4m/13 × 13ft

Skimmia japonica
'Rubella' Red buds open to white flowers.
E, 1.5 × 1.5m/5 × 5ft

Osmanthus delavayi
Plant to appreciate the wonderful scent of this shrub. E, 3 × 3m/ 10 × 10ft

EARLY CLEMATIS

It is not just their lovely colours but the nodding habit of their flower heads which make the alpina and macropetala clematis so appealing. On the left is *C. alpina*, on the right *C. macropetala* 'Blue Bird'.

These are clematis to scramble into the lower branches of trees and shrubs, to tumble over low retaining walls or to grow in pots and containers. Pruning is simply limited to removing unwanted growth and cutting out any weak or dead stems.

***Clematis macropetala* 'Markham's Pink'** These sugary pink flowers look gorgeous with many of the spring flowering bulbs. 1.8m/6ft

◆ *Macropetala and alpina clematis do equally well in both sun or partial shade although the former do prefer a shadier aspect.*

TENDER PERENNIALS
Many border perennials which are inclined to be tender are best left until now to be cut back.

Among those perennials which would benefit from this treatment are all the penstemons, diascias, hardy fuchsias and border osteospermums.

Illustrated here is *Penstemon glaber*. This is one of the smaller growing penstemons, enjoying a long flowering season from early summer onwards. E, ○, 60 × 60cm/2 × 2ft

DIVISIONS
Herbaceous perennials in need of division which were not tackled in March may still be lifted and divided this month.

April is by tradition the time of year when asters, Michaelmas daisies, are divided. *Aster novi-belgii* 'Goliath', shown here, will flower from late summer into autumn in an open, sunny situation. ○, 1.2m × 45cm/4 × 1½ft

PLANTING EVERGREENS

April is an ideal month in which to plant evergreen trees and shrubs.

Dig a hole which is large enough to accommodate the roots of the plant and line the base with a good measure of planting compost. Before removing the plant from its container, or unpacking the root ball if ball-rooted, water well.

Insert a stake and then place the plant in position. Tease out any tangled roots and infill with planting medium. Firm down to eliminate pockets of air but do not compact. Keep watered in dry periods.

SOW HARDY ANNUALS

Hardy annuals, like this clarkia, may be sown during April in open ground where they are to flower.

With a few exceptions, hardy annuals require very little in the way of specially cultivated or enriched soil.

Once germination has occurred, seedlings should be thinned out.

PROTECT SEEDLINGS
Spring crops are particularly vulnerable to decimation by birds. The protection of netting, or even thread criss-crossed over the crop, is advised.

During the month check the setting of fruit and spray if necessary against pests and diseases.

THE KITCHEN GARDEN
Sowing should begin in the open on fairly dry soil which has had time to warm after winter. In order to obtain a succession of vegetables, and to avoid gluts, it is wise to sow successive small quantities so that crop may follow crop. Always sow in drills rather than broadcast seed. Water if the weather is dry, especially whilst seedlings are tender.

Outdoors, the following may be sown: broad beans, beetroot, carrots, chicory, leeks, lettuce, spring onions, parsley, parsnip, peas, radish, spinach and Swiss chard. Of the brassicas, broccoli, cabbage, kale, swede and turnip may all be sown. Aubergine, French beans, celery, sweetcorn and outdoor tomatoes will need to be sown in heat or under protection.

Finally, artichokes, main-crop potatoes and strawberry runners may be planted out.

CULTIVATING ASPARAGUS
Asaparagus beds should occupy a sunny, open position. Soil should be deeply dug incorporating copious amounts of strawy manure.

One or two year-old crowns should be obtained and planted during this month. Roots should be spread out and covered in good soil. Plants should be set in rows about 30cm/1ft apart. Dress in early spring each year with well rotted dung.

PROPAGATING DAHLIAS
The easiest method of propagation is to place overwintered tubers in March or April in shallow boxes of moist compost in a warm place. Quite quickly a number of strong shoots should appear. Detach these and set out in pots to grow on. After one season, treat as old tubers.

CHECK LIST

- Lift and divide polyanthus after flowering (p.44).
- Cultivate spring flowering alpines for the rock garden (p.48).
- Top dress camellias (p.54).
- Complete bare root plantings (p.56).
- Cut back tender perennials (p.58).
- Divide asters (p.58).
- Plant evergreen trees and shrubs (p.59).
- Sow hardy annuals in situ (p.59).
- Sow vegetable seeds (p.60).
- Establish an asparagus bed (p.61).
- Propagate dahlias (p.61).
- Prune early-flowering shrubs like *Berberis*, *Forsythia* and *Spiraea* immediately after flowering.
- Prune less hardy shrubs like *Ceanothus*, *Fuchsia*, *Hydrangea*.
- Mulch beds to help eliminate weeds and conserve moisture.

PLANTING WATER LILIES
Aquatic planting baskets are the easiest means.
Planting depths depend upon size. Miniature lilies may be planted in 23cm/9in of water and small-growing ones in 30cm/1ft. Medium-growing lilies will need up to 45cm/1½ft, the most vigorous 1m/3ft.

MAY

Thalictrum aquilegiifolium Mauve, pink or white frothy flowers are carried above ferny foliage. 1.2m × 60cm/4 × 2ft

MAY is one of the loveliest of months. The magic of spring peaks and everywhere gardens rejoice in a surfeit of colour. Borders, previously pocketed with bare soil, burgeon with the unstoppable growth of perennials many of which, until now, have had life checked by the uncertainties and vagaries of April weather. This is the month of those splendid fillers, forget-me-nots, honesty, grannies' bonnets which, left to seed, contribute to an air of plenty and fullness to which all gardeners aspire. Weeds remain a potential problem. They will, unless seriously arrested with hoe or hand fork, take hold.

Aquilegia vulgaris Columbines should be allowed to seed throughout the border. Following flowering (and seeding if required), cut to ground level. Within a short time a fresh mound of foliage will appear. Look out for named varieties such as 'Nora Barlow' and 'Magpie'. 1m × 45cm/ 3 × 1½ft

A beautifully co-ordinated, colour-themed May border. Drifts of forget-me-nots are complemented by taller growing columbines whilst the Welsh poppy, *Meconopsis cambrica*, provides a yellow accent. This picks up the gold of the hosta leaves and will as surely tone with the *Hemerocallis*, which is about to flower.

Armeria maritima
Thrift will grow in poor soil provided it is given reasonable drainage.
○, E, 10 × 20cm/4 × 8in

Saxifraga × urbium
London Pride can make a splendid edging. E, 30 × 30cm/1 × 1ft

***Phlox carolina* 'Bill Baker'** An invaluable, early flowering phlox. 30 × 30cm/1 × 1ft

Lunaria annua alba, white honesty, Welsh poppies and faithful forget-me-nots combine here to give a flavour of the traditional cottage garden. All these hardy annuals and biennials are self-sown and once established in the garden require little, if any, attention.

Euphorbia polychroma
Bracts of greenish-
yellow rise above a
mound of foliage.
45 × 60cm/1½ × 2ft

Euphorbia griffithii
'Fireglow' Keep watch,
for this euphorbia likes
to run. ○, 1m × 75cm/
3 × 2½ft

Lunaria annua alba Biennial white honesty
sparkles wherever it chooses to place itself.
1m × 45cm/3 × 1½ft

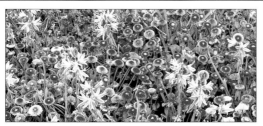

***Bellis* 'Medici Rose'** is
partnered with star of
Bethlehem.
15×23cm/6×9in

◆ *Schemes like this need to
be planned so that plants
have time to establish.*

Centaurea montana
Cornflowers are always
deserving of a place.
45×60cm/$1^{1}/_{2} \times 2$ft

PLANTING FOR EFFECT
Experience shows that
blocks, or ribbons, of
the same plant in a
border are a certain
way of creating impact.
Contrasts, either of
colour, form or texture,
are likely to be all the
greater if plantings are
generous and carried
out with at least a sense
of plenteous abandon.
   This planting of
Veronica gentianoides
'Tissington White'
underlines the idea.
45×45cm/$1^{1}/_{2} \times 1^{1}/_{2}$ft

Gentiana acaulis
Unforgettable, deep
blue flowers.
◑, E, 10 × 15cm/4 × 6in

***Viola soraria* 'Freckles'** Exquisite white violets,
delicately freckled with lavender. 10 × 30cm/
4in × 1ft

Libertia formosa Apart
from a need for good
drainage, libertia will
flourish in either sun or
part shade.
E, 90 × 60cm/3 × 2ft

Smilacina racemosa
This is a plant to
enliven a shady area. At
the season's end cut
leaves back to ground
level. ◑, 75 × 75cm/
2½ × 2½ft

Trillium grandiflorum roseum Trilliums need
humus rich, moist, well-drained, acidic, or at least
neutral, soil in a shady situation. ●, 40 × 30cm/
1ft 4in × 1ft

Primula sieboldii
Lightly fringed,
unusually veined
flowers which range in
colour from pale blue,
through white and pink
to dark red. Plant in a
cool, moist spot with a
little shade.
15 × 15cm/6 × 6in

Dicentra spectabilis Bleeding heart is the name by which this perennial is widely known. 60 × 45cm/2 × 1½ft

◆ *'Alba', a white form, is worth growing as well. Both are content in either a sunny place or a partly shaded one.*

Hesperis matronalis
Sweet rocket is short lived but may be relied upon to seed around freely. Seedlings vary from white to lilac, but all are scented.
◑, 75 × 60cm/2½ × 2ft

Thermopsis montana
makes a good border
perennial. 75 × 75cm/
2¹/₂ × 2¹/₂ft

Mertensia virginica
This unusual plant
needs good drainage.
◑, 60 × 45cm/2 × 1¹/₂ft

Limnanthes douglasii
The poached egg plant
will readily seed about.
○, 15cm/6in

***Geum rivale* 'Leonard's Variety'**
Although commonly known as water
avens, geum will succeed in most
ordinary garden soil. 45 × 45cm/
1¹/₂ × 1¹/₂ft

◆ *G. rivale 'Lionel Cox' is a highly
desirable hybrid of soft primrose with
a hint of apricot. G. rivale 'Album' is
an equally attractive white form.*

BULBS AND TUBERS

Late-flowering tulips, amongst them beautifully fringed parrots, elegantly shaded *viridiflora* and exciting paeony types, complement the herbaceous plants which are currently filling beds and borders. In addition, the first of the showy alliums, camassias and lily-of-the-valley underline the continuing importance of bulbous plants to the overall spring display. From midsummer onwards bulbs are on offer for sale both in garden centres and through nursery catalogues; the earlier in the season, the wider the choice. Later, planting should be undertaken throughout the autumn to be completed by Christmas. Go around the garden now, notebook in hand. Gaps in borders may be noted, and sympathetic choices made.

Paeonia arietina
Flowers of this free-growing plant vary from deep to light magenta-pink or, exceptionally, to pale rose-pink. Peonies appreciate humus-rich soil. 75 × 60cm/2½ × 2ft

IRISES IN MAY
Among the spring flowering irises are those known as Intermediate Bearded Irises. Grown in full sun, and given well drained soil, they should flower freely.

Shown here are Californian hybrid irises. These grow to between 30 and 60cm/1–2ft and are coloured from deep purple to white.

Tulipa **'Noranda'**
Blood-red petals, tinted
orange at the edges.
45cm/1½ft

◆ *For early May, choose
'Blue Heron', 'Fringed
Beauty' or 'Maja'.*

Tulipa **'Black Parrot'**
One of the most striking
of all parrot tulips.
45cm/1½ft

Tulipa **'Spring Green'** Green shaded
petals are the hallmark of the
delicately coloured, superbly elegant
viridiflora tulips. 45cm/1½ft

◆ *Stronger mixes, each striped
green, are to be found in the
varieties 'Golden Artist',
'Hollywood' and 'Pimpernel'.*

Shown here are 'China Pink' tulips underplanted with forget-me-nots. Such a scheme amply illustrates the effectiveness of generous plantings which achieve their impact through a limited range of colour.

Hyacinthoides non-scriptus Bluebells should be restricted to less formal areas. 45 × 30cm/1½ × 1ft

Allium aflatunense **'Purple Sensation'** White lychnis and pink forget-me-nots provide a subtly coloured carpet for the striking heads of this cultivated form of onion. 1m/3ft

Rhodohypoxis baurii Grow these in peaty soil dressed with horticultural grit. ○, 5cm/2in

Camassia leichtlinii In the wild these hardy, bulbous plants are to be found in moist grasslands. Obtain bulbs in the autumn and plant to a depth of 5cm/2in to form clumps in a border which does not dry out. 75 × 30cm/ 2½ × 1ft

Convallaria majalis A place for lily-of-the-valley should be found in every garden on account of the beautifully fragrant flowers. They are, in fact, totally unfussy. Plant in well composted soil, then allow to increase. ◑, ●, 20cm/ 8in

SHRUBS AND TREES

Late spring sees them possibly at their best as new leaves unfurl and previously bare branches are ripe with blossom. Indeed, the spring flowering almonds, cherries and crabs are one of the chief delights of the season and their continued popularity is completely understandable.

Much enjoyment may be had by planning planting schemes to complement these flowering trees and shrubs. Neighbouring bulbs and perennials, even annuals, may be deliberately chosen to contrast with or reflect the same colour tones.

Aesculus neglecta **'Erythroblastos'** This slow growing tree delights in the spring with new leaves of shrimp pink.
○, 10 × 10m/33 × 33ft

Malus × *schiedeckeri* **'Red Jade'** Later on the branches of this tree will be laden with deep red crab apples. In spring it is a profusion of pink and white blossom.
4 × 6m/13 × 20ft

◆ *For bright yellow fruits, and an otherwise similar habit although not weeping, grow* M. × zumi *'Golden Hornet'.*

***Sorbus aria* 'Lutescens'** Shimmering new leaves appear white felted. As they develop throughout the summer, so the colour changes to grey-green. Whitebeams are hardy, of easy cultivation, suitable as windbreaks and tolerant of chalk. $10 \times 10m/33 \times 33ft$

***Prunus* 'Kanzan'** Something a little softer, such as *P.* 'Hokusai' or *P.* 'Pink Perfection', may be preferred. For pure white, *P.* 'Tai Haku' is near perfect. 8 × 8m/26 × 26ft

Cercis siliquastrum The Judas tree is smothered in small pea-like flowers in mid-spring followed by red pods later. It is deciduous, fully hardy but best planted in a sunny position. ○, 10 × 10m/33 × 33ft

Spiraea **'Arguta'** Stems wreathed in white give rise to the name bridal veil. 2.4 × 2.4m/8 × 8ft

Choisya ternata will flower again later (see p. 214). E, 2 × 2m/ 6 × 6ft

Cytisus × *kewensis* A spreading broom for the rock garden. ○, 45cm × 1.5m/1½ × 5ft

Exochorda × *macrantha* **'The Bride'** Weeping stems bearing conspicuous paper-white flowers sweep downwards in late spring. 'The Bride' is unsuitable for growing on chalk; an alternative would be *E. koroikowii*. ○, 2.4 × 3m/8 × 10ft

Here the darkly flushed leaves of *Weigela florida* 'Foliis Purpureis' are balanced with the upright habit of *Syringa* 'Antoine Buchner' and the twiggy growth of *Cotoneaster horizontalis*. Both the weigela and lilac will flower around the same time whilst the cotoneaster will be bright with berry in autumn.

Clematis montana White flowers mark the true montana. Pink flowered varieties, often referred to as montana, are all named forms. All are capable of growing to several metres depending on soil, type and aspect.

***Clematis* 'Nelly Moser'** An accommodating clematis, with its cartwheel effect of mauve-lilac bars on the petals. ◐, 2.4m/8ft

◆ *Flowers, repeated in late summer, will fade if planted in sun.*

***Ceanothus* 'Blue Mound'** Ceanothus are amongst the loveliest of shrubs. Sadly, not all are entirely hardy. ○, E, 1.5 × 2m/5 × 6ft

◆ *In a very cold area try* C. × thyrsiflorus *which is generally regarded to be one of the hardiest varieties.*

Halesia monticola The snowdrop tree
will thrive in full sun, moist, free-
draining soil which is acid or neutral.
○, 6 × 4m/ 20 × 13ft

◆ *For a rose-coloured flower,
rather than white, grow* H.
monticola *'Rosea'*.

Convolvulus cneorum
This shrub is tender and
needs a sheltered, well
drained, sunny spot. ○,
E,1 × 1.2m/3 × 4ft

Paeonia delavayi var.
ludlowii All the tree
peonies are handsome
shrubs. 2.4 × 2.4m/
8 × 8ft

Paeonia suffruticosa
'Situfukujin' Forms of
'Moutan Paeony' are
widely available.
2.4 × 2.4m/8 × 8ft

For those with acidic soil the growing of rhododendrons presents no problems. They are ideal subjects to form a backdrop to a border, garden or even landscape. Illustrated above are two of the more compact types, 'Golden Torch' and 'Sneezy'.

Rhododendron Azalea **'Hino-mayo'** A free flowering, compact form, 'Hino-mayo' would make a container plant. E, 1.5 × 1.5m/5 × 5ft

Rhododendron Hybrid **'Blue Star'** A pleasing contrast to pinks and yellows. E, 1.5 × 1.5m/ 5 × 5ft

May represents the main flowering period of rhododendrons (and
azaleas). Top left is the dwarf, evergreen Hybrid 'Peeping Tom' whilst
on the right is Azalea 'Palestrina', a white flowered evergreen
growing to 1.2m/4ft. Bottom right is *R. yakushimanum* which will
reach 1.5m/5ft. On the left is *R.* Azalea 'Hino-mayo', height 1.5m/5ft.
In the centre is the evergreen Hybrid 'Elizabeth', 1.2m/4ft.

Rosa **'Frühlingsgold'**
Long-reaching stems,
scented flowers.
2.2 × 2m/7 × 6ft

Rosa rugosa **'Alba'** This
rose is seldom without
flower throughout the
summer. 2 × 2m/6 × 6ft

Rosa xanthina **'Canary
Bird'** The first roses of
summer are special.
'Canary Bird' is
amongst the earliest to
flower and its cheerful
canary-yellow blooms
above fresh, ferny
foliage are especially
welcome. 2.2 × 2.2m/
7 × 7ft

Rosa hugonis Soft,
primrose-yellow flowers
along gracefully arching
branches. 2.2 × 2m/
7 × 6ft

Fremontodendron mexicanum is best trained as a wall shrub. ○, E, 6m/20ft

Genista lydia Golden flowers completely cover this rounded shrub. 60 × 60cm/2 × 2ft

Fothergilla major Scented white flowers appear before the leaves. 3 × 3m/10 × 10ft

Few would deny the magnificence of a laburnum tunnel on this scale.

***Laburnum* × *watereri* 'Vossii'** (*right*) may be grown as a specimen tree. A word of caution – all parts of the laburnum are poisonous. 10 × 10m/ 33 × 33ft

Wisteria floribunda A well-grown wisteria will almost certainly excite interest. ○, 9m/30ft

◆ *A curtain of white will be achieved by growing* W. floribunda *'Alba'. For scent, look to the sinensis forms. In summer, prune long side-growth back to four or five leaves. In winter, shorten back to two buds.*

THE WATER GARDEN

It is generally agreed that one of the most difficult aspects of maintaining a pond is keeping the water clear.

Oxygenating plants, either floating or submerged, will aid healthy conditions.

Fish, too, serve a practical as well as decorative purpose. The introduction of goldfish, common carp, rudd and roach will assist in the control of insect pests.

Encouraging wildlife, in the form of frogs, toads, newts and dragonflies, is yet another way in which a natural balance may be sustained and problems minimized, if not eliminated.

Aponogeton distachyos
Water hawthorn. Plant up to a depth of 45cm/1½ft.

Myriophyllum aquaticum Parrot's feather flourishes just beneath the surface of the water.

Orontium aquaticum
Apart from its oxygenating properties, this is an attractive plant in its own right. The whole plant should be placed in 30cm/1ft of water.

PLANTING POTS FOR SUMMER

Felicia amelloides Blue
marguerites look
positively splendid in
pots. Felicia is not
hardy. 45 × 30cm/
1½ × 1ft

Now is the time to start filling all manner of
containers in preparation for the months to
come. It matters little what is used,
providing allowance is made for drainage.
Always allow room for roots to expand but
not too much as this will leave areas of earth
which will simply go 'stale'. The compost, or
growing medium, should be suited to the
plant, perhaps lime-free as in the case of
lime-hating plants, and it pays to cover the
surface of the pot when planted with a layer
of horticultural grit; this will look smarter,
help conserve moisture and minimize
disturbance of the soil.

Aeonium arboreum
Brought outside for the
summer months, the
tender aeonium
contributes both style
and variety.

***Abutilon
megapotamicum*** Not
completely hardy.

A simple handcart utilized as a plant container. By
limiting the material to white marguerites, pink
pelargoniums and trailing lobelia a sense of unity
and purpose is achieved.

Hanging baskets form a traditional part of summer displays. Line the basket and fill with compost, water retentive granules and a fertilizing agent.

Plant up the basket, tucking plants into holes made in the sides. Set aside in a sheltered place. Keep watered.

The completed basket is ready for hanging out. Baskets dry out very easily. Water daily, twice daily in hot weather.

As the summer progresses, apply a nitrogen feed to keep the basket looking good into autumn.

Fuchsia **'Red Spider'** Pendulous
fuchsias are ideal to be included in
hanging baskets or containers.

Fuchsia **'Mrs. Churchill'** Although it
is reluctant to branch out, this
fuchsia has been used on its own
most successfully in a hanging pot.

Clashing colours
combine in this window
box to make a startling
but spirited display.
Petunias of shocking
pink are mixed with
red pelargoniums,
orange nemesia and
blue and white lobelia.

A colourful
arrangement of
begonias mixed with
mauve flowered
pelargoniums is the
mainstay of this window
box. In addition to
flower colour, the
begonias add a sense of
luxuriance with their
shapely, glossy leaves.

STAKING
Successful border management depends on effective staking if tall growing
perennials are to keep their shape and withstand the vagaries of the
weather. Here the tall-growing cardoon, *Cynara cardunculus*, is supported
with bamboo canes and string.

HARDY BIENNIALS

Seed of hardy biennials like forget-me-nots, foxgloves (shown on the right), honesty, sweet williams and wallflowers should be sown in prepared seed drills this month. By autumn they should be of sufficient size to transplant into beds and borders.

Alternatively, as with hardy annuals, they may be sown directly into the positions where they will flower and any excess plants can then be thinned out.

HALF-HARDY ANNUALS

Half-hardy annuals, sown in March (see page 39), should now be ready for planting out. Naturally this should be delayed if there is any risk of frost.

DAHLIAS

Dahlia tubers, overwintered in a frost free environment, may now be set out.

Tubers should be planted about 1m/3ft apart. They should remain in situ until the first frosts of autumn.

Tagetes patula French marigolds remain a popular choice.
○, 30 × 30cm/1 × 1ft

Salvia splendens Trail a blaze of colour with this bedding salvia.
○, 30 × 30cm/1 × 1ft

***Gazania* 'Dorothy'** Gazania flowers close up when out of the sun.
○, 20 × 20cm/8 × 8in

SUMMER BEDDING

Glorious displays in the months ahead owe their success, in part, to preparation and planning taking place now. Hardy annuals, sown in position in April, should be starting to get away and to these may be added half-hardy ones.

Bedding schemes may be strictly colour themed or mixed, depending on personal taste and requirements. Whatever, it is important to keep new plants well watered to encourage root growth.

KITCHEN GARDEN
To the main crops sown previously may be added Brussels sprouts, cauliflower, courgette (zucchini), cucumber, endive, fennel, peppers, runner beans and sweetcorn (maize). Seeds which have come through, thin where necessary. This particularly applies to root crops.

CLIP HEDGES
Quick-growing or ornamental hedges, such as box, may be trimmed in the late spring to retain their shape.

CHECK LIST

◆ Maintain a programme of weeding (p.62).
◆ Plant perennials for maximum effect (p.66).
◆ Note gaps to be filled with bulbs for next year (p.71).
◆ Control algae on ponds (p.89).
◆ Plant up pots for summer colour (p.90).
◆ Fill hanging baskets (p.92).
◆ Stake tall-growing perennials (p.94).
◆ Sow seed of hardy biennials (p.95).
◆ Plant out half hardy annuals (p.95).
◆ Set out dahlia tubers (p.95).
◆ Complete summer bedding (p.96).
◆ Continue sowing of vegetable seeds. Thin root crops (p.97).
◆ Trim ornamental hedges (p.97).
◆ Keep pests and diseases under control. Spray against greenfly and rose blackspot. Renew slug pellets.

STRAW STRAWBERRIES
Just before the flowers of the strawberry plants open, hoe the ground thoroughly and then cover with fairly short straw.

JUNE

WITH THE ONSET OF JUNE, spring slips quietly away and summer, the glory of the garden, gathers pace. This is the month of wonderfully fragrant roses, of cascading clematis, and of borders over-spilling with favourite flowers – campanulas, delphiniums, dianthus, irises, oriental poppies and sweetly smelling violas. Tasks are no longer onerous, rather routine. Constant dead heading, a pleasure on a warm evening, seldom a chore, results not only in well manicured borders but assists in prolonging the flowering period. Lawns mown regularly, and edges trimmed, present a crisp background to floral displays. Spring-flowering perennials cut to the ground will very quickly throw up a mound of fresh, new foliage, possibly a bonus flower or two.

Geranium endressii **'Wargrave Pink'** All of the hardy geraniums, or cranesbills, flower over many weeks. 60 × 60cm/2 × 2ft

Geranium sanguineum var. *striatum* Pale pink flowers tone with many herbaceous perennials. ○, 30 × 45cm/1 × 1½ft

Generously stocked borders provide a continuous flower display over several months. In the foreground liberal plantings of pink dicentra, flowering from May, spill out onto the path to mask an otherwise straight edge. Complementing these is a ribbon of *Gladiolus byzantinus*, the daring colour of which purposely draws the eye along and picks up the tones of the hardy geranium. Mauve nepeta, planted at intervals, acts as a foil to predominantly pink shades.

Scabiosa caucasica
Scabious thrive on any
fertile soil. ○,
60 × 60cm/2 × 2ft

Summery aquilegia in shades of pink and violet-
blue happily mix here with rose-coloured silene
and aromatic nepeta.

In this border flag irises are partnered with gladiolus, peonies and hardy
geraniums. To succeed, the iris should be planted in a position where their
rhizomes receive full sun. Every three or so years, following flowering, lift
plants and divide overcrowded rhizomes.

Primula helodoxa The strong colour of this species primula picks up the tone of the yellow flag, *Iris pseudacorus*. 60 × 45cm/2 × 1ft

Alchemilla mollis The lady's mantle is surely without equal as a foil. 60 × 60cm/ 2 × 2ft

Lupinus polyphyllus Easily raised from seed, lupins are amongst the brightest of June flowers and are available in a wide range of colours, including many named forms. In a mixed border plant behind later perennials to avoid gaps once the flowering period is over.

Dianthus **'Pike's Pink'**
Border pinks begin
their long flowering
period in June. All
require good drainage.
○, E, 15 × 15cm/6 × 6in

A low wall like this may be planted up to
provide a tapestry of colour from
springtime into summer. Although the
purple aubrieta is now virtually
over, awaiting shearing back, the
cheerful yellow *Corydalis lutea*,
seen on the left, will continue
to flower for many weeks to
come.

Centranthus ruber
Commonly known as
valerian, centranthus
flowers in shades of
pink, red and white and
is a prolific self seeder.
1m × 45cm/3 × 1½ft

Enjoying the free draining site is
the helianthemum, rock rose. This
small spreading shrub is to be
found in a wide range of
colour and is in bloom from
late spring onwards.
Variegated London
pride, *Saxifraga*
'Aureopunctata',
forms fleshy,
evergreen
rosettes.

***Paeonia officinalis* 'Rubra Plena'** A double peony for cottage gardens. 60 × 60cm/ 2 × 2ft

Papaver orientale Red is the traditional colour of oriental poppies. 1m × 60cm/3 × 2ft

***Penstemon* 'Red Knight'** Tubular flowers of the hardier hybrids appear continuously from June until October. ○, E, 75 × 45cm/2½ × 1½ft

***Helianthemum* 'Supreme'** To keep the rock roses in good shape they should be cut back fairly severely once the flowering period is over. To neglect this will result in straggly plants which become very woody. ○, E, 15 × 45cm/6in × 1½ft

Lychnis chalcedonica Startling red flowers, true vermilion and somewhat difficult to place, appear from early summer and look best massed together. Maltese cross enjoys a sunny place in the garden and will stand up better with some support if wind is a problem. 1m × 45cm/3 × 1½ft

This summer scheme relies on two principal players. In the foreground are the spherical, purple heads of the ornamental onion, *Allium aflatunense* (1.2m × 30cm/4 × 1ft), whilst further back are ethereal spikes of *Asphodelus albus* (1m × 30cm/3 × 1ft).

Stachys macrantha These purplish-pink flowers belong to a hardy herbaceous perennial with dark leaves carried on erect stems. 45 × 45cm/1½ × 1½ft

Baptisia australis An unusual and lovely plant. 75 × 60cm/ 2½ × 2ft

Iris missouriensis Damp soil is a requirement of this handsome lavender-blue iris. For this reason a bog garden or the margins of a pond would provide the correct environment. 60 × 60cm/2 × 2ft

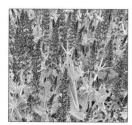

***Salvia* × *superba* 'Mainacht'** A good front-of-border plant. 60 × 30cm/2 × 1ft

Polemonium reptans Jacob's ladder, to be found seeding in all old gardens, is, like aquilegia, useful as a filler in a mixed border. 30 × 45cm/1 × 1½ft

***Geranium pratense* 'Mrs Kendall Clark'** This attractive pale form of the meadow cranesbill will form useful clumps. 75m × 45cm/2½ × 1½ft

Lilium martagon Turk's cap lilies are wonderful in grass.
◗, 1.5m × 30cm/5 × 1ft

Gillenia trifoliata Flights of graceful white flowers float over sparsely leaved, red stems on this unusual herbaceous perennial. 1m × 60cm/ 3 × 2ft

◆ *Gillenia would look particularly charming rising from a carpet of the little white violet,* Viola cornuta alba.

Imagine this border scheme in the twilight with the ethereal beauty of all these whites made so much more intense by the gathering darkness. Holding centre stage is the lovely, single peony, 'White Wings', supported by white aquilegias, foxgloves, some a soft apricot, foaming sprays of *Crambe cordifolia* and nodding heads of *Viola cornuta alba*.

Asphodeline lutea Straw yellow flowers among hide-coloured bracts. 1m × 60cm/3 × 2ft

◆ *Slightly later, and a rather paler yellow, is* A. liburnica.

Cephalaria gigantea Soft primrose yellow flowers. 2 × 1.2m/6 × 4ft

Centaurea macrocephala The rich buttery flowers surrounded by brown parchment bracts make a bold and sunny statement. To extend the scheme of yellow, plant *C. macrocephala* alongside the new English rose, 'Graham Thomas'. 1m × 60cm/3 × 2ft

Campanula latiloba
'Hidcote Amethyst'
Divide every three or so
years to maintain virile,
healthy plants.
1.2m × 30cm/4 × 1ft

Hosta sieboldiana Grow
hostas for their bold,
dramatic foliage; their
flowers are, in
comparison, less
significant. ◑,
75 × 75cm/2½ × 2½ft

Delphiniums No June border should be without
these tall-growing, floriferous herbaceous
perennials available in a wide range of colours.
1.5m × 60cm/5 × 2ft

'Marguerite Hilling'
Warm-pink blooms on
this rose. 2.4 × 2.2m/
8 × 7ft

'Pink Bells' A very
pretty ground-cover
rose for a sunny bank.
60cm × 1.2m/2 × 4ft

'Ballerina' Of all the
dwarf polyantha roses,
'Ballerina' is amongst
the best known.
1.2 × 1m/4 × 3ft

'Buff Beauty' Hybrid
musk roses are noted
for the fragrance of
their flowers and this
one is no exception.
1.5 × 1.5m/5 × 5ft

'Gertrude Jekyll' One
of many English roses
which may be relied
upon for their robust
habit, abundance of
flowers and disease free
foliage. 1.2 × 1m/
4 × 3ft

MODERN SHRUB ROSES

Sensuous roses confirm the presence of
early summer. This arrangement of *Rosa*
'Mary Rose', hardy geraniums and scented
violas illustrates one of the ways in which
the modern shrub roses may be easily
incorporated into a garden scheme.

'Tuscany Superb'
Wonderful, velvety
blooms. 1.5 × 1m/5 × 3ft

OLD SHRUB ROSES

Gallica, Damask, Alba, Centifolia and Moss,
such names conjure up a real spirit of the
past, of the Medes and the Persians, of the
Crusaders and the Romans, of the dark and
mysterious Middle Ages. For these are the
roses of history, of forgotten centuries.
Richly scented, magnificent blooms typify
these lovely lax shrubs.

'Madame Zoetmans'
Damask roses were
originally cultivated for
attar, rose oil.
1.2 × 1m/4 × 3ft

♦ *Among the Damask
roses are the 'Celsiana',
'Gloire de Guilan',
'Ispahan' and 'Kazanlük'.*

'Variegata di Bologna'
Fully cupped,
deliciously scented
blooms. 1.5 × 1.2m/
5 × 4ft

♦ *Other Bourbon roses are
'Madame Pierre Oger',
'Reine Victoria' and
'Souvenir de la
Malmaison'.*

'Madame Isaac Pereire' Of all the Bourbon roses this must surely rank among the loveliest. 2 × 1.5m/6 × 5ft

◆ *When pruning any shrub rose, aim for a nicely open framework by removing all congested growth.*

'Comte de Chambord' One of the Autumn Damask Roses. 1.2 × 1m/4 × 3ft

***Rosa* 'Mundi'** (*Rosa gallica versicolor*) Blooms are heavily scented. 1.2 × 1.2m/4 × 4ft

◆ *Grow* Rosa *'Mundi' as a low, compact hedge.*

Coppery tints of *R.* 'Edith Holden', partnered here with the pink and buff of *R.* 'Iced Ginger', hold together this modern planting scheme. In the background *Iris* 'Perryhill' is teamed with the scarlet bells of *Penstemon barbatus*.

MODERN BUSH ROSES

For sheer brilliance of bloom, for innovative colour, for massed display, the modern bush rose will satisfy all such demands. Included in this group are the Hybrid Teas, multi-flowered Floribundas, and an extensive range of Miniature and Patio roses, many ideal for small gardens or pots.

'Royal William' A succession of fragrant, velvety-crimson blooms. 1 × 1m/3 × 3ft

'Iceberg' flowers over a long period, often well into winter. 1.2 × 1.2m/4 × 4ft

'Sweet Dream' Bushy, upright growth and dense foliage make this apricot-peach, patio rose suitable for the rock garden or for pot cultivation. 45cm/1½ft

'Queen Elizabeth' An exceptionally vigorous, strongly growing rose. 1.5 × 1m/5 × 3ft

'Madame Alfred Carrière' A vigorous Noisette climber. 3.5 × 3m/12 × 10ft

CLIMBING ROSES

The Climbing and Rambler roses may be put to endless use. Combine them with a complementary clematis for an eye-catching display of colour and interest over the summer period.

From the past come much-loved 'Climbing Cécile Brunner', 'Gloire de Dijon' and 'Zéphirine Drouhin' whilst among the more modern are 'Compassion', 'Danse du Feu' and 'Schoolgirl'.

'Blush Noisette' An absolutely enchanting rose. This is the original Noisette producing a continuous display of semi-double, pink-white flowers, flushed with lilac, from summer until autumn. As a bonus the blooms are deliciously scented, smelling of cloves. 2.2m/7ft

◆ *Of similar habit are the silky lemon 'Céline Forestier', modern coral-pink 'Dreamgirl', crimson 'Gruss an Teplitz' and bronze-yellow 'Maigold'.*

'Paul's Himalayan Musk' Surely one of the most beautiful of ramblers. 9m/30ft

'New Dawn' Vigorous, fragrant and tolerant of some shade. 3.5m/12ft

'Albéric Barbier' The double flowers of this sturdy rambler open creamy white. 6m/20ft

'Félicité et Perpétue' Distinctive pompom flowers mass this classic rambler rose throughout the flowering season. 3.5m/12ft

CLIMBING AND RAMBLER ROSES

Climbing roses possess larger flowers than those to be found on ramblers, more closely resembling those of other garden roses. Generally they are likely to repeat their flowering whereas the ramblers flower mainly once only. The stems of climbing roses are stiff and are generally retained as a framework whilst ramblers have lax stems.

'Empress Josephine' A truly magnificent old French rose which will be in flower towards the end of June and early July, a period when the garden is really dominated by roses. 1.2 × 1.2m/4 × 4ft

SHRUBS IN JUNE

June brings with it a succession of flowering shrubs many of which, like the mock oranges, lilacs and lavenders, are wonderfully scented.

Climbers continue to contribute a well furnished look to the garden and in early summer there is no shortage of richly coloured clematis, delicate solanums, exotic passion flowers and sweet smelling honeysuckles from which to make a choice. Remember too the evergreen ivies, many lustrous with brightly variegated foliage.

Solanum crispum **'Glasnevin'** In a mild garden this wall-trained shrub will climb to 6m/20ft or more. ○, E or semi-E, 6m/20ft

***Clematis* 'Ernest Markham'** This is a strong growing clematis. Best in full sun. 4m/12ft

◆ *Advice on pruning clematis is given on page 26.*

***Clematis* 'Niobe'** Display these velvety, ruby-red flowers against a variegated shrub, such as an aucuba, elaeagnus or holly. 3m/10ft

Lavandula stoechas Use lavenders to line a path, edge a border, as a low hedge, or simply for fragrant colour in a mixed bed. E, 1 × 1m/3 × 3ft

(*Opposite*) Silver leafed perennials act as a foil to the papery white flowers of the sprawling cistus which, in turn, is highlighted against a haze of blue ceanothus. This is a refreshingly cool scheme to counteract the hot days of summer. The cistus, planted in full sun and given sharp drainage, will delight for weeks to come. Beds or borders, or parts of, planted in a similar manner are, importantly, restful in their own right.

× **Halimiocistus** Given a hot, dry situation this charming little shrub will reward with a profusion of flowers from the late spring well into summer. E, 60cm × 1.2m/2 × 4ft

Hydrangea anomala subsp. **petiolaris** Greenish-white, flat headed flowers held in large clusters will cover a mature plant of this self-clinging hydrangea in June. Once established this is a vigorous climber. 8 × 1m/26 × 3ft

Cornus kousa Small, cream flowers are followed in the autumn by most unusual, strawberry-like fruits. Known as the Chinese dogwood. 3.6 × 4m/12 × 13ft

Cistus × hybridus Sun and good drainage are essential if this low growing shrub is to reward with a succession of flowers over a long period. Flower buds are tinted crimson before opening white. ○, E, 1 × 1m/ 3 × 3ft

Abutilon × *suntense* This
deciduous shrub will
have been in flower
from April in a warm,
sunny situation. Prune
hard previous season's
growth in early spring.
○, 5 × 3m/15 × 10ft

Philadelphus **'Belle Etoile'** Mock oranges are
beautifully scented shrubs for the June border.
'Belle Etoile' is one of the best. ○, 2.4 × 2.4m/
8 × 8ft

Clematis **'Marie
Boisselot'** This elegant,
white-flowered clematis
should be found a place
in every garden. Should
it exceed its allotted
space, or become
tangled, cut back to
ground level in spring.
3.5m/7½ft

***Kalmia latifolia* 'Nimuck Red Bud'** For those who garden on anything other than acidic or, at worst, neutral soil, the cultivation of *Kalmia* will prove an unequal struggle. The calico bush is a splendid, evergreen shrub.
E, 3 × 3m/10 × 10ft

Rosa glauca Striking grey-green foliage acts as a foil to small, pink flowers. 2 × 1.2m/6 × 4ft

Neillia thibetica Considering the ease of cultivation, it is surprising that this attractive shrub is not more widely grown. Flowers from April onwards. 2 × 2m/6 × 6ft

Lonicera periclymenum
'Belgica' Should be
permitted to scramble.
7m/23ft

Kolkwitzia amabilis
'Pink Cloud' The
graceful beauty bush.
3 × 3m/10 × 10ft

Deutzia × elegantissima
'Rosealind' A really
pretty June shrub.
1 × 1.5m/3 × 5ft

Lavatera **'Barnsley'** This is a shrub for an open,
sunny spot in free-draining soil. Given these
conditions it will flower profusely for several
months. 2 × 1m/6 × 3ft

Lupinus arboreus These
are easily propagated
from seed. Semi-E,
1.5×1.5m/5×5ft

***Brachyglottis* (*Senecio*)
'Sunshine'** This shrub
forms a compact dome.
○, E, 1×1.5m/3×5ft

Buddleja globosa
Inflorescences on this
early-flowering buddleja
are unmistakably
scented. 2.4×2m/8×6ft

Phlomis fruticosa The Jerusalem sage carries
whorls of brilliant yellow flowers from early
summer onwards. Here it is teamed with
Campanula poscharskyana. E, 1×1m/3×3ft

Rosa '**Blanc Double de Coubert**' Flowers for most of the summer. 1.5 × 1.2m/5 × 4ft

Abutilon vitifolium '**Album**' Unsuitable for exposed gardens. ○, 2.4m/8ft

Carpenteria californica Bright, glossy foliage and beautifully scented white flowers with pronounced golden anthers in June and July. ○, E, 1.5 × 1.5m/5 × 5ft

Clematis '**Mrs. Cholmondeley**' Hard prune this clematis in the spring to promote lavender-blue flowers from early summer. Suitable for a pot or container. 3m/6ft

Buddleja alternifolia An exceptionally attractive shrub. Grow in a mixed border or as a specimen. ○, 4 × 4m/13 × 13ft

GARDENS OPEN TO THE PUBLIC

Succumb to the temptation during these long days of summer to abandon working in the garden in favour of visiting one of many open to the public.

For the price of a small admission charge, often for charity, countless gardens, open to visitors during the summer months. This is a wonderful opportunity to gain ideas, to discover new plants or simply to seek relaxation.

The formal design of this garden relies on total symmetry of hard and soft landscaping, both artfully controlled, to achieve its effect. Clever use is made of topiary, not only in the form of the golden balls but in the way in which the clipped spirals echo the pillars of the little summerhouse.

Here late summer perennials extend the season after the main June display.

Colours in this mixed border are thoughtfully combined to create a unified whole.

This long vista invites the visitor to explore, the archway in the distance acting as a magnet. Softly textured roses contrast with tightly clipped yew.

Illustrated here is just a small part of a much larger garden. However, it is often possible to adapt ideas and scale to fit a much smaller space.

THE KITCHEN GARDEN
Successional sowings of salad crops on a fortnightly basis will give a constant supply through the summer into autumn.

Cabbage and celeriac may be planted out this month.

Cutting from established asparagus beds should be discontinued from the middle of the month.

WATERING
Essential watering, carried out when the sun is down, should be applied directly, if at all possible, to the roots of each plant and not over foliage.

Plants in pots must, of course, receive regular watering and should never be allowed to dry out. In very hot periods, move them out of the sun.

SOW FOR NEXT YEAR
By June the ground should be sufficiently warm to allow for the sowing of herbaceous perennials and hardy biennials not sown in May.

Sow seed in drills, cover lightly and water using a fine rose. Within a few weeks seedlings should be large enough to thin out and transplant.

If required, hardy biennials like the *Dianthus barbatus*, sweet William, shown here may be sown where they are to flower.

SOFTWOOD CUTTINGS
Early summer is an ideal time in which to propagate shrubs, like this potentilla, by softwood cuttings.

Sturdy shoots should be removed from the plant and a clean cut made just below a joint. Remove or shorten excess leaves.

Cuttings should be arranged around the edge of a pot containing an appropriate compost mixture.

Water well and place in a cold frame in a shady situation. As cuttings strike, increase ventilation, harden off and pot up individually.

CHECK LIST

◆ Regularly dead head to prolong flowering period.
◆ Continue to cut and edge grass.
◆ Visit garden centres and nurseries to purchase new plants in flower (p.107).
◆ Check stakes of tall-growing perennials like delphiniums.
◆ Add colour to terrace or patio with Miniature or Patio roses in pots (p.117).
◆ Introduce additional climbers into the garden (pp.118 and 121).
◆ Visit gardens open to the public for inspiration (p.130).
◆ Sow herbaceous perennials for next year (p.132).
◆ Make fortnightly sowings of salad crops (p.132).
◆ Take softwood cuttings of shrubs (p.133).
◆ Check roses for pests and diseases. Spray if necessary.
◆ Prune late-spring flowering shrubs like *Kerria*.

TIDY BORDERS
Maintenance of borders – dead heading, cutting back, weeding and checking stakes – will ensure that the garden remains looking good.

JULY

MIDSUMMER, and the July garden is awash with colour. This is the month of red hot pokers, of flat headed yarrow, of long-flowering penstemons and diascias, of garden pinks and tall, border phlox. Summer bedding reaches a new intensity. Vibrant reds, golden yellows, indeed all the strong colours of the palette, combine to reflect the heat of the sun in this the hottest of months.

This is a month in which to relax, to enjoy not only the richness of the borders but also the delicious scents of summer.

These parallel borders, seen in the early days of July, give an appearance of extravagant plenty whilst being very tightly controlled in terms of colour and plant mix. Large clumps of lime-green alchemilla and purple sage are used at intervals with confidence.

***Epilobium angustifolium album/Lavatera* 'Barnsley'** A very effective combination. White rosebay willow herb is teamed in this garden with the shrubby mallow to provide an interesting contrast of flower shape as well as colour. 1.2m × 60cm/4 × 2ft and 2 × 1m/6 × 3ft

Verbena bonariensis The low-growing shrub *Lavatera* 'Burgundy Wine' is encircled here by a haze of airy *Verbena bonariensis*. This tall, slender stemmed perennial will flower from July until October. 1.2m × 15cm/4ft × 6in

Penstemon '**Apple Blossom**' enjoys good drainage and full sun. ○, 45 × 45cm/1½ × 1½ft

Campanula punctata '**Rubriflora**' This is a very striking campanula. 30 × 30cm/1 × 1ft

◆ *Similar in form is* C. takesimana *but flowers are mottled, wine red over white.*

Osteospermum jucundum will form a spreading mat. ○, 30 × 30cm/1 × 1ft

Alstroemeria **hybrid** This rather shocking pink alstroemeria makes a spectacular display. ○, 60 × 30cm/2 × 1ft

◆ *'Ligtu hybrids' are to be found in colours to suit most tastes.*

Monarda '**Cambridge Scarlet**' Spidery flowers are carried above strongly aromatic leaves. ○, 1 × 1m/3 × 3ft

Anthemis tinctoria **'Alba'** Repeated dead heading will encourage continuous flowering of this sun-loving perennial. ○, 75 × 75cm/2¹/₂ × 2¹/₂ft

Eryngium tripartitum Blue and spiky flowers on this sea-holly. ○, 45 × 25cm/1¹/₂ft × 10in

Aster × frikartii **'Mönch'** will add colour for months. ○, 75 × 45cm/2¹/₂ × 1¹/₂ft

Convolvulus sabatius A charming addition to a gravel garden. Not completely hardy. ○, 15 × 45cm/6in × 1¹/₂ft

Lysimachia punctata Lysimachia will thrive in most situations. 75 × 75cm/2¹/₂ × 2¹/₂ft

◆ *Look out for* L. ciliata *'Firecracker' whose foliage is a deep burgundy red.*

SCENTED PLANTS

Capture the perfumes of Arcadia by filling the July garden
with scented plants. Fragrant pinks, heady lilies, tobacco
plants, sweet-smelling stocks, lavender and southern-
woods, each delights individually and together they
contribute to a midsummer pot-pourri.

Dianthus '**Waithman**
Beauty' A pink which is
small enough to include
in the rock garden. ○,
E, 15 × 23cm/6 × 9in

Lilium candidum Who
can resist the purity,
and heavenly scent, of
the Madonna lily? ○,
1.2m/4ft

◆ *By growing lilies in*
containers, they may be
moved into a prominent
position for their flowering
period.

Pots of *Lilium regale* and tender
Acidanthera bicolor murielae are
placed here among
lavenders and pinks to
surround this seat
with lovely
summer
fragrances.

COLOUR WHEEL
Adjacent colours, and
those opposite each
other, will go together.

SUMMER SCHEMES – *White and Blue*

Borders in which the principal colours are restricted to one, two or possibly three, have a special appeal. Experimentation with colour is endless. White gardens are firmly established in present day garden lore. Combining blue and white together, in varying degrees, is to modify a familiar theme and, by the thoughtful arrangement and juxtaposition of plants, is to break new ground.

***Phlox paniculata* 'White Admiral'** From late July into August and beyond this cool twinning of scented phlox and dark blue agapanthus, *Agapanthus* 'Loch Hope', will provide startling yet controlled border colour. 75 × 60cm/2½ × 2ft

Campanula alliariifolia
A rather dreamy
campanula. This
perennial prefers moist
soil. ☽, 75 × 45cm/
2½ × 1½ft

Eryngium bourgatii This
sea-holly provides
texture and form. ○,
60 × 30cm/2 × 1ft

Campanula persicifolia
White, blue and double
forms. ○, 1m × 30cm/
3 × 1ft

***Campanula
poscharskyana*** An
indispensable rockery
campanula which will
spread about into
cracks and crevices. It
will continue flowering
until the frosts arrive.
25 × 60cm/10in × 2ft

***Solanum jasminoides*
'Album'** Introduce this
climber as a backdrop.
◯, Semi-E, 6m/20ft

Salvia patens The
bright blue flowers are
almost without equal.
◯, 60 × 45cm/2 × 1½ft

***Lathyrus latifolius*
'White Pearl'** Sweet
peas are essential. ◯,
2m/6ft

***Veronica austriaca* 'Shirley Blue'** Plant either in groups or arrange as a
ribbon to thread through a white border. 'Shirley Blue' has a tendency to
flop a little so is excellent where informality is the order. ◯, 20 × 30cm/
8in × 1ft

Campanula latiloba alba Cool white bell flowers create a moody, enticing atmosphere when placed in a lightly shaded spot. Use this campanula as a mainstay of a white border. *C. latiloba* is studded with lavender-blue flowers. 1.2m × 30cm/4 × 1ft

SUMMER SCHEMES – *Red and Yellow*

Recent years have seen much emphasis on pale pastel schemes, so a return to something more vibrant is challenging. Fiery, hot borders are increasingly fashionable and when flaming annuals are added to perennials, then the garden is truly ablaze.

Abutilon megapotamicum A spectacular shrub to grow against a warm wall in full sun. Conspicuous, and rather strange, red and yellow flowers which appear from early June could not be bettered for a hot scheme. Numerous garden hybrids are obtainable. ○, E, 2.4m/8ft

Potentilla fruticosa A cheery little shrub. 1.2 × 1.2m/4 × 4ft

Callistemon rigidus This is a shrub for a well drained, acidic soil in full sun. ○, E, 3m/10ft

Hypericum calycinum The buttery yellow flowers of Rose of Sharon. E, 30cm/1ft

Tropaeolum speciosum Plant this splendid climber with its brilliant scarlet flowers to grow against a dark background. Here it climbs into a yew hedge. By the time the hedge needs cutting, the flowers will be over. 2m/6ft

Tropaeolum majus
Garden nasturtiums are
fast-growing annuals. ○,
30 × 30cm/1 × 1ft

***Canna* 'Fireside'**
Intensely dramatic
cannas. ○, 75 × 30cm/
2½ × 1ft

***Penstemon* 'Chester
Scarlet'** This
penstemon has proved
to be reliably hardy. ○,
60 × 45cm/2 × 1½ft

Lilium pardalinum A planting of leopard lilies with
their nodding turkscap flowers will revel in the
summer sun. ○, 2m × 30cm/6 × 1ft

A hot border such as this one will be alight from early
summer right through until autumn. The last
rose, 'Just Joey', contrasts with the flat heads of
achillea whilst the red and orange
crocosmias will remain in flower for
weeks. The round blooms of the
dahlia are partnered with the
tassels of amaranthus.

SUMMER SCHEMES – *Lemon and Purple*

Purple, in isolation, may appear somewhat oppressive, dowdy even, so that in a small area the overall effect could be one of dullness and general gloom. Add yellow, from the palest of tints to deep lemon, and the border is electrified.

Washed out yellow hollyhocks, *Alcea rugosa*, intermingle with *Penstemon* 'Alice Hindley', whilst the deeper shades of *Clematis* 'Perle d'Azur' reinforce this deliberately restricted colour scheme. Bracts of *Euphorbia amygdaloides* var. *robbiae* are in complete harmony.

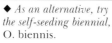

Oenothera **'Fireworks'** A fairly compact perennial evening primrose. ○, 45 × 30cm/1½ × 1ft

◆ *As an alternative, try the self-seeding biennial,* O. biennis.

Clematis × *durandii* Deep indigo flowers throughout July and August. 2.4m/8ft

Helichrysum italicum with catmint and magenta geranium. ○, 60 × 60cm/2 × 2ft

Clematis **'Victoria'** Rosy-purple *Clematis* 'Victoria' and the day lily, *Hemerocallis* 'Whichford'. 3.5m/12ft

Kniphofia **'Little Maid'** An excellent plant for introducing variation in form. These creamy-yellow pokers are well suited to the small garden. 60 × 45cm/2 × 1½ft

Scrambling through and beyond the climber
Rosa 'Golden Showers' are the rich purple
flowers of the vigorous *Solanum crispum*
'Glasnevin', whose yellow central points pick
up exactly the tones of the rose. Not only is
the rose scented, but so too are the madonna
lilies which surround it.

Lonicera tragophylla In
total contrast to the
solanum, this warmly
coloured honeysuckle
will happily climb and
flower in total shade.
Unfortunately the
delightfully formed
flowers are without
scent. ●, 6m/20ft

SUMMER BEDDING

By July summer bedding, in place now for several weeks, should be filling out to provide an ongoing display. Schemes planned over several months mature by midsummer. During prolonged dry spells it may become necessary to water shallow-rooted bedding plants.

A series of raised beds has been used here as home to a range of bedding plants. These include impatiens, nicotiana and ageratum, all arranged in linear composition.

Nicotiana enjoy a sunny situation where they will flower all summer. ○, 30 × 15cm/1ft × 6in

***Chrysanthemum
parthenium*** Most
suitable for edging. ○,
23 × 15cm/9 × 6in

Antirrhinum
Snapdragons are
favourite plants. ○,
30 × 15cm/1ft × 6in

Impatiens Free
flowering busy lizzie will
tolerate some shade.
30 × 15cm/1ft × 6in

A carefully co-ordinated arrangement.
Chrysanthemum parthenium is used to edge the bed
with *Salvia splendens* and impatiens weaving a ribbon
of colour around evergreen conifer and hebe.

***Argyranthemum*
'Vancouver'** For
informal situations. ○,
1 × 1m/3 × 3ft

Centaurea cyanus Grow
cornflowers to self-seed.
○, 45 × 15cm/
1½ft × 6in

Heliotrope Strongly
scented flowers over
dark green leaves. ○,
45 × 15cm/1½ft × 6in

Contrast of colour, variation of height, carefully arranged drifts are the
principal ingredients of this very attractive border.

In the main plants are restricted to triphylla fuchsias and *Argyranthemum*
'Jamaica Primrose'. Neither will, of course, withstand frost.

The tall-growing
Nicotiana
'Sensation' and
the large
double flowers
of zinnia in
an informal
bedding
scheme.

***Rosa filipes* 'Kiftsgate'** Where space is unlimited this wonderful white rose, with individual shoots of 6m/20ft or more, will create an amazing, breath-taking cascade of flower in midsummer. Not, it should be stressed, for anywhere other than a huge area.

SHRUBS AND TREES

Scent remains a dominant force among the trees and shrubs of July.
From wonderfully fragrant honeysuckles, among them the common
Lonicera periclymenum, to aromatic lavenders and the pineapple-
scented *Cytisus battandieri*, there is something for every garden.

***Lonicera periclymenum* 'Serotina'** An exceedingly attractive honeysuckle with
an enticing perfume which will succeed in both sun or part shade in any
ordinary garden soil. As an alternative, choose *L. × americana* which is
equally scented. 7m/23ft

Indigofera heterantha
Place this compact
shrub in a hot, dry spot.
○, 2 × 2m/6 × 6ft

Hebe The summer-
flowering hebes will
delight. E, 45cm × 1m/
1½ × 3ft

Lavandula angustifolia
'Hidcote' One of the
best lavenders. ○, E,
60 × 45cm/2 × 1½ft

Lavatera maritima bicolor The unusual flower colour of this tree mallow is
very appealing. Flowers appear on the current season's growth so all stems
should be hard pruned to the ground in spring. 2 × 1m/6 × 3ft

Cytisus battandieri
Beautifully scented
flowers. Semi-E,
5 × 5m/16 × 16ft

Sorbaria tomentosa var.
angustifolia Elegant
white plumes.
3 × 3m/10 × 10ft

Escallonia 'Iveyi' 'Iveyi'
is best afforded a little
shelter from winter
winds. E, 4 × 3m/
13 × 10ft

Genista aetnensis The Mount Etna broom is a
mass of sunny flowers at this time and would be
splendid at the back of a border. 4 × 4m/13 × 13ft

CONTAINERS

Pots and containers planted up in May are now satisfying all their past promise. Lilies in particular are made for pot cultivation. By growing them in containers they may be given the good drainage they demand, water during the growing season and, not least, the prominence which is their due when in flower.

Begonia semperflorens **'Kalinka Rose'** may be sited in sun or shade. 60cm × 1m/2 × 3ft

An old lead cistern has been utilized here as a home for pelargoniums and a purple leafed cotinus. The pelargoniums will be changed annually but the shrub may remain.

White petunias and blue lobelia enhance the simple dignity of this stone trough.

Schizanthus A very pretty pot arrangement using a popular annual.

Care has been taken in this welcoming sitting-out area to keep plants in pots of similar tones. This reinforces a feeling of restfulness.

Cheery pansies are teamed up in this trough with lobelia to give a long lasting summer display.

This stone urn has been filled with a white argyranthemum.

Agave americana The succulent century plant with its sharp, sword-like leaves is not, sadly, hardy. Housed over winter in a frost-free environment, it takes pride of place for the season in a small, enclosed court. 1 × 1m/3 × 3ft

Fuchsia **'Tennessee Waltz'** This makes a magnificent pot specimen. ◑, 1m × 75cm/3 × 2½ft

Brugmansia Angel's Trumpet makes an impressive plant. 1.2 × 1m/4 × 3ft

Fuchsia **'Rufus the Red'** The flowers are produced in profusion during season. ◑, 1.5m × 75cm/5 × 2½ft

Lilium **'Stargazer'** Of all the oriental hybrid lilies, the popularity of 'Stargazer' is never in question. Upright crimson-red flowers, a spicy fragrance and long-lasting blooms are the qualities which have proved its worth. 1.2–2m/4–6ft

Lilium **'Mont Blanc'**
Plant in clumps of three, five, seven or more for a better display.
75cm–1m/2½–3ft

Lilium regale Sweet scent and elegant flowers flushed yellow. 1.2–2m/4–6ft

Lilium **'Pink Perfection'** Large trumpet flowers of deep pink. 1.5m/5ft

163

THE PONDSIDE

More than at any other time of the year, this part of the garden now enjoys a feeling of plenty, made possible by generous plantings of ferns, grasses, hostas, rushes, as well as flowering meadowsweet (*Filipendula*), day lilies (*Hemerocallis*) and late irises.

Bold drifts of astilbes and irises around this pond ensure continuous colour. *Iris pseudacorus* (Yellow flag) has finished flowering but the odd *I. sibirica* keeps going. The main display is of white *Astilbe* 'Deutschland' with pink *A.* 'Erica' behind.

Effective planting demonstrating a variety of form and texture. The foliage of tall, strappy irises contrasts with the pink flowered astilbes behind. The bronze form of the sedge *Carex comans* softens the edge of the path.

Ferns, hostas and summer primula, *Primula florindae*, are the mainstays of this scheme for the margins of a pond. Golden leaves of *Carex elata* 'Aurea' artfully pick up the same colour tones of the primula.

Deep red plumes of *Astilbe* 'Montgomery' make a bold, dramatic statement in this planting scheme around a narrow stream. In winter both foliage and flowers will have died down to reveal the water.

***Hemerocallis* 'Bonanza'**
Day lilies are tolerant of most situations.
1m × 75cm/3 × 2½ft

***Zantedeschia aethiopica*
'Crowborough'** needs very damp conditions.
60 × 60cm/2 × 2ft

Ligularia przewalskii At home in any garden soil which is moisture retentive. This is a spreading perennial so allow ample space. 1.2 × 1m/4 × 3ft

Primula florindae
Flowers of this moisture-loving primula carry a distinct scent. ◑,
75 × 75cm/2½ × 2½ft

Rodgersia pinnata
'Superba' This plant is
excellent for foliage.
1 × 1m/3 × 3ft

Polygonum affine
'Superbum' Use this as
a carpet. 20 × 30cm/
8in × 1ft

Primula vialii An
unusual primula for
damp soil. 30 × 30cm/
1 × 1ft

Filipendula rubra
'Venusta' Meadowsweet
is an excellent plant for
the water's edge.
1.5m × 75cm/5 × 2½ft

◆ Filipendula purpurea
alba *is an attractive white
form for any damp
situation.*

THE KITCHEN GARDEN
Onions and shallots should soon be ready to harvest. Before doing this, bend the tops over to prevent seeding and to allow for maximum sunlight on the onions themselves.

Other jobs include cleaning and tidying strawberry beds and summer pruning of fruit trees.

Continue successional sowings of crops like beetroot, summer lettuce, radish, salad onion, spinach. These should mature before the first frosts but are likely to be the last crops that do so.

DRYING HERBS AND FLOWERS
Gather herbs and flowers for drying during a warm period. Cut stems cleanly, arrange in thin bunches and hang upside down in an airy place at an even temperature to dry.

PROPAGATION BY LAYERING

July is the usual month for propagating by this easy, sure method.

Make an upward cut just below a joint on a lower stem. This incision should open the stem to about the centre. Peg it down and pile soil over, firming well. The outer end of the shoot should be trained upwards.

When the layer has rooted it should be cut away and planted out.

LIFT SPRING BULBS

Spring bulbs, such as daffodils and tulips, will have now died down. These may be lifted, if required.

CHECK LIST

- ◆ Arrange scented plants in pots on patio or terrace (p.138).
- ◆ Consider colour theme borders (pp.140–151).
- ◆ Continue programme of dead heading.
- ◆ Feed and water summer bedding (p.152).
- ◆ Attend regularly to container-grown plants (p.160).
- ◆ Dry herbs and flowers for decorative use (p.168).
- ◆ Harvest onions and shallots (p.168).
- ◆ Clean up strawberry beds (p.168).
- ◆ Summer prune fruit trees (p.168).
- ◆ Continue successional sowings of vegetables (p.168).
- ◆ Propagate by layering (p.169).
- ◆ Lift spring bulbs (p.169).

ATTEND TO ROSES

Dead head and tidy rose bushes and then apply a general fertilizer. This should keep them in good condition.

AUGUST

HIGH SUMMER and holidays. August is a time of transition, a link
between the secure days of summer and the onset of autumn. But
borders need not be dull. Already late flowering perennials are
making a show and colourful annuals have many weeks yet to run.
Temperatures often remain high and inevitably some plants will
show signs of being under stress. Water only if absolutely essential,
and then ensure that water is sufficient to reach and saturate roots.
Lawns may well be parched and brown. This should not cause
concern for the first of the autumn rains will quickly restore them
to their original colour and vitality.
Weeds should no longer present much of a problem.

An enthusiastic mix of annuals and perennials results in a bright display
which will remain looking good right into autumn. Fuchsias, petunias,
orange crocosmias, tagetes and dahlias are but a few of the many plants
which contribute to this scene.

Helianthus **'Monarch'** Sunflowers are fun to grow and look very splendid soaring upwards at the back of a border. ○, 2.1 × 1m/7 × 3ft

Dendranthema **'Nathalie'** A chrysanthemum. 90cm/3ft

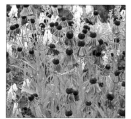

Helenium **'Moerheim Beauty'** Long-lasting flowers. ○, 1m × 60cm/ 3 × 2ft

Crocosmia **'Mount Usher'** All crocosmias prefer a sunny site. ○, 60 × 30cm/2 × 1ft

Alcea rosea Hollyhocks have always had a place in the cottage garden. Available in a wide range of colours, including near black. 2m × 60cm/6 × 2ft

Lobelia cardinalis **'Queen Victoria'** These intense red flowers are in bloom for several weeks. ○, 90 × 30cm/3 × 1ft

Fuchsia magellanica **'Gracilis Variegata'** A hardy fuchsia. 75 × 75cm/2½ × 2½ft

Liatris spicata **'Kobold'** A very pretty perennial for the later part of the summer. 60 × 45cm/ 2 × 1½ft

All too often hardy fuchsias are overlooked for inclusion in the late summer border. Their availability in colours from the softest to the richest makes them suitable for virtually any scheme and they flower for weeks on end.

In this border the red and purple flowers of *Fuchsia* 'Mrs. Popple' complement the deep blue of *Aconitum carmichaelii* and tone with the sombre leaves of the purple sage.

This particular bedding scheme, which makes use of brightly coloured African marigolds to surround a young monkey puzzle tree, *Araucaria*, will remain as dazzling as this until the first of the frosts.

Calendula Marigold is an easy summer bedding plant. Thrives on poor soil. ○, 45cm/1½ft

Tagetes erecta Double ball-shaped blooms typify African marigolds. ○, 75cm/2½ft

Petunia Petunias are useful for bedding, window boxes, pots and hanging baskets. ○, 15–45cm/6in–1½ft

Acanthus spinosissimus
Purple hooded bracts.
○, 1.2m × 75cm/
4 × 2½ft

Clematis heracleifolia
'Wyevale' Treat this as
any other perennial.
1 × 1m/3 × 3ft

Sedum **'Ruby Glow'**
provides continuous
colour at this time. ○,
30 × 30cm/1 × 1ft

Echinops **'Taplow Blue'** An impressive stand of the globe thistle planted as a
drift through the back of this predominantly blue border. Globular flower
heads may be as large as 7½cm/3in across. 1.5m × 60cm/5 × 2ft

Providing necessary height at the back of the border is *Tamarix ramosissima*. Central to the arrangement is a bold clump of *Phormium tenax* with its distinctive, sword-like leaves, the whole surrounded by a rugosa rose. Far right, *Fuchsia* 'Riccartonii' flowers alongside *Escallonia rubra* 'Crimson Spire'.

All of the plants surrounding this inviting seat are suitable for growing at the seaside. Coastal gardens, usually much milder than those inland, are subject very often to strong, salt-laden winds capable of damaging all but the most stalwart of plants. For this reason the planting of a shelter belt becomes of strategic importance.

SHRUBS AND TREES

Late flowering trees and shrubs contribute a wide range of colour to the August garden.

Koelreuteria paniculata
(*left*) Pride of India or Golden rain tree are two of the names given to this handsome, medium-sized tree which bears panicles of small, yellow flowers during August.
13 × 8m/43 × 26ft

***Eucryphia ×
nymansensis*** This highly ornamental tree should be protected from cold winds. E, 14 × 4m/ 46 × 13ft

Hydrangea aspera (syn. *villosa*) One of the loveliest of all the lace-cap hydrangeas. Plant in a semi-shaded spot in acidic or neutral soil. Hydrangeas, both mop-head and lace-cap, need moisture at the roots. 2.4 × 2m/8 × 6ft

Hydrangea macrophylla 'Veitchii' Suitable for most garden soils as lime-tolerant. 2 × 2.7m/ 6 × 9ft

Hydrangea macrophylla 'Hamburg' On more acidic soils the colour will deepen to purple-rose. 2 × 2.4m/6 × 8ft

Hydrangea macrophylla 'Ayesha' Hydrangeas make excellent shrubs for containers. 1 × 1.5m/3 × 5ft

Yucca gloriosa One of the most architectural of plants. Grow in pots or containers or to provide a statement of form in the border. E, trunk to 2m/6ft – flower to 2.4m/8ft

Perovskia atriplicifolia **'Blue Spire'** A graceful shrub, the Russian sage should be hard pruned to ground level in spring. 1.5 × 1m/5 × 3ft

Itea ilicifolia Long, drooping flower racemes. Grow against a warm wall. E, 3 × 3m/ 10 × 10ft

Caryopteris × clandonensis A similar effect to perovskia and requiring the same pruning treatment. ○, 80 × 80cm/2½ × 2½ft

***Aralia elata* 'Variegata'**
A mature example of
the Japanese angelica
tree is, understandably,
highly prized. 3.5 × 3m/
12 × 10ft

***Hibiscus syriacus* 'Blue Bird'** These single violet-
blue flowers cover this shrub during August and
September. ◯,2 × 2m/6 × 6ft

***Ceanothus* × *delileanus* 'Gloire de Versailles'**
From July onwards a mature bush is heaped with
light powder blue panicles of flowers. 2 × 2m/
6 × 6ft

***Magnolia grandiflora*
'Exmouth'** will grow to
be a large tree. E,
10 × 10m/33 × 33ft

Buddleja davidii Not surprisingly this type of buddleja is referred to as the butterfly bush for butterflies flock around it during summer. Hard pruned in spring, it grows rapidly to flower on the current season's growth. 4 × 4 m/13 × 13ft

Clematis viticella **'Purpurea Plena Elegans'** Grow through a small shrub. 3.5m/12ft

Clematis texensis **'Etoile Rose'** Best when allowed to scramble into a shrub. 2m/6ft

Clematis viticella **'Etoile Violette'** Imagine this deep purple flower in association with a golden leafed shrub.

Schizophragma integrifolium Use this ornamental climber to cover an old tree stump or to grow against a wall. Creamy white flowers are produced in July and August. ○, 6m/20ft

Polygonum baldschuanicum Russian vine will smother any structure very rapidly. ○, 12m/39ft

THE KITCHEN GARDEN

From the middle of the month begin successional sowings of spring cabbages for winter harvest. After six weeks, or thereabouts, plants should be ready for transplanting.

Winter lettuce may be sown from August until October.

SEMI-RIPE CUTTINGS

New shoots are ideal to take as cuttings during August and September.

Choose sturdy, half mature side shoots and make a straight cut below a joint. Remove any leaves from the lower half. Dip the bottom of the cutting into hormone rooting powder and insert around the side of a pot filled with a suitable cutting compost. By spring plants should have rooted.

GROWING DAHLIAS

Dahlias are easily grown in open ground. In very warm districts they may be left to overwinter in position. More often, though, tubers are lifted.

When this happens, cut off all but about 15cm/6in of stem and hang, stem down, to dry completely. Plunge into a box of sand and store free from damp, frost and heat.

PRUNE SUMMER-FLOWERING SHRUBS

Shrubs, like deutzia, philadelphus and weigela, indeed those which have flowered during the months of June, July and the beginning of August may be pruned now or as soon as they have finished flowering.

Shorten any exceptionally long shoots above a bud, then remove about one third of the oldest stems.

Now should also be the time to prune Rambler roses – that is, when they have finished flowering. Prune all stems that have flowered to ground level. Train and tie in new shoots.

PLACE BULB ORDERS

As spring bulbs begin to appear in garden centres, now is the time to place orders.

CHECK LIST

- ◆ Water any plants showing signs of stress (p.170).
- ◆ Include hardy fuchsias in late summer borders (p.173).
- ◆ Consider hydrangeas for pot cultivation (p.179).
- ◆ Cultivate dahlias for colour into autumn (p.184).
- ◆ Make sowings of winter cabbage and lettuce (p.184).
- ◆ Take semi-ripe cuttings (p.184).
- ◆ Prune summer-flowering shrubs, including Rambler roses (p.185).
- ◆ Order spring bulbs (p.185).

CLIP HEDGES

This is the month to trim hedges and to shape topiary. Clip hedges to encourage a well furnished look to the ground.

Create a warm
welcome beside an
entrance with an
arrangement of pots
for late summer.
Included here are
brugmansia (datura),
canna and phormium.

SEPTEMBER

ALTHOUGH September sees the beginning of autumn, more often than not the days remain pleasantly warm and are, in reality, an extension of summer.

Japanese anemones, one of the treats of the later part of the year, are in full flower now and are accompanied by late pokers, rudbeckias and the first of the main show of asters.

Attention to detail will keep the garden fresh and interesting in the weeks ahead. Continued dead heading, the cutting back of summer perennials are all on-going tasks.

This late September border draws on *Verbena bonariensis*, asters and the purple cone flower, *Echinacea purpurea*, for autumn colour. In the background, glimpsed through the verbena, is the yellow daisy, *Rudbeckia fulgida* 'Goldsturm'.

All of the Japanese anemones will add grace and charm to end of season borders. Shown here is the pink *Anemone hupehensis* 'September Charm'. Other cultivars include purplish pink *A.h.* 'Hadspen Abundance', white *A. × hybrida* 'Honorine Jobert' and the mid-pink *A. × h.* 'Königin Charlotte'. Most grow in ordinary garden soil to around 1.5m/5ft.

Aconitum carmichaelii A rich blue, tall-growing perennial. 1.5m × 30cm/ 5 × 1ft

Kniphofia caulescens Dramatic torch-like flowers. ○, 1m × 60cm/ 3 × 2ft

Schizostylis coccinea Kaffir lilies thrive best in a damp situation. 60 × 30cm/2 × 1ft

Aster thompsonii **'Nanus'** The flowering period of this small, lilac aster extends from midsummer well into autumn. 45 × 25cm/ 1½ft × 10in

Aster novi-belgii **'Lilac Time'** and *Aster novi-belgii* **'Jenny'** Normally these Michaelmas daisies will be unlikely to start flowering until the end of the month.

Kirengeshoma palmata For successful cultivation, plant in semi-shade in humus-rich soil which is moisture retentive. ◑, 1m × 75cm/3 × 2½ft

Aster luteus Tiny, pale canary-yellow daisies cover this pretty aster. 60 × 30cm/2 × 1ft

***Arctotis × hybrida* 'Apricot'** A tender plant. ○, 45 × 30cm/ 1½ × 1ft

Helianthus Young children will delight in growing sunflowers from seed. ○, 2.1 × 1m/ 7 × 3ft

Senecio tanguticus Eye-catching perennial for the back of the border. 1.5m × 60cm/5 × 2ft

Gypsophila Fill gaps with frothy pink or white flowered gypsophila. 1.2 × 1.2m/ 4 × 4ft

***Rudbeckia fulgida* 'Goldsturm'** A wonderful autumn perennial. Black-eyed daisies will flower right through autumn and even into winter if the weather is kind. Plant in blocks for maximum impact. ○, 75 × 45cm/2½ × 1½ft

SHRUBS AND TREES

The approach of autumn brings with it a second flowering, albeit intermittently, of a number of the shrubs whose main flowering period is much earlier in the year. Of these many of the roses may be relied upon to provide a second flush of bloom. Late clematis prolong the season.

Leycesteria formosa Beetroot-coloured bracts enclose the tiny flowers of this shrub. Stems should be reduced to ground level in spring. 2 × 2m/6 × 6ft

***Rosa moyesii* 'Geranium'** Early flowers of blood-red are followed by these startling heps which decorate the long, arching stems in autumn. 2.4 × 2.2m/8 × 7ft

Clerodendrum bungei
Flowers are borne on
fresh stems.
1.2m × 30cm/4 × 1ft

Buddleja crispa One of
the most desirable of all
buddlejas. ○, E, 1 × 1m/
3 × 3ft

◆ *Plant in a very sheltered
spot.*

An early autumn planting. Central to the scheme is a bold clump of *Heuchera*
'Rachel' whose dark leaves contrast with the prettily shaped, grey-green
leaves of *Geranium renardii*. *Fuchsia magellanica* 'Gracilis Variegata' is a mass of
flower.

These two splendid clematis, flowering at the same time from July until September, are ideal companions. The pearly-white flowers of *Clematis* 'Huldine' show up well against the deep velvety blooms of *C. viticella* 'Royal Velours'.
'Huldine' will reach around 5m/16ft whilst 'Royal Velours' is slightly less vigorous at 3.5m/12ft. Other viticella hybrids of comparable size for a similar situation are 'Margot Koster' and 'Venosa Violacea'.

***Clematis* 'Rouge Cardinal'** Rich magenta flowers appear from June until the end of September. It prefers a sunny, south-facing position. 2.4–3m/8–10ft

***Clematis × eriostemon*
'Hendersonii'** Allow to
stray through the
border. 2.4m/8ft

Clematis rehderiana
Delightful, fragrant
flowers. 2.4–3m/8–10ft

***Clematis* 'Lasurstern'** Flowers first in May and
June and then again in August and September.
The second flowering may be slightly less prolific.
3m/10ft

Clematis tangutica
Yellow lantern-like
flowers typify this
rampant species
originating in China.
Flowers continue well
into autumn. 5m/16ft

Hedera helix
'Buttercup' A golden-leafed form of ivy which should be grown in full sun. E, 2.7m/9ft

Parthenocissus tricuspidata **'Veitchii'** The wonderful autumn foliage of the Boston ivy deepens to claret-red. 20m/66ft

Humulus lupulus **'Aureus'** Yellow leaves of this sprawling form of hop will brighten the dullest days. 4m/13ft

TRANSPLANT EVERGREENS

The start of autumn is a good time in which to move evergreen trees and shrubs.

Prepare the planting hole to the correct size in advance and insert a stake to steady the new planting.

Insert into the new position and back fill with well rotted garden compost. Water well.

PLANT BULBS FOR SPRING

Bulbs which have been offered for sale since August may be planted during this month.

Begin with crocuses, daffodils, hyacinth, scillas and winter aconites. Tulips are better left until October.

ESTABLISH A NEW LAWN

Warm September rains make this month an ideal time in which to establish new lawns, either from seed or using turf. Seed should be sown evenly at a rate of 50g/2oz per square metre/yard. After sowing, soil should be given a very light raking.

Before laying turves rake the surface of the ground. Place turves in such a manner that they will bond and sieve soil into any gaps. Water and lightly roll until the lawn is durable.

DIVIDE AND REPLANT IRISES

Where iris rhizomes have become overcrowded, they should be divided. Normally this takes place after flowering. September is a suitable month in which to carry this out although the job could be put off until October.

SOW ANNUALS FOR SPRING

Very hardy annuals sown now, as opposed to those sown in the spring, will bloom much earlier.

Sown in trays, and then transplanted and potted on, they may be kept over winter in a cold greenhouse.

CHECK LIST

◆ Continue general garden maintenance (p.187).
◆ Plant late-flowering clematis for seasonal colour (pp.194–5, 196).
◆ Establish a new lawn (p.198).
◆ Transplant evergreens (p.198).
◆ Plant spring bulbs (p.198).
◆ Divide irises (p.199).
◆ Sow hardy annuals for spring (p.199).
◆ Move pots of tender plants, like pelargoniums (also known as geraniums) and fuchsias, indoors before first frosts (p.211).

AUTUMN PLANTING
Warm soil, more certain rainfall and workable ground make this an excellent season for planting perennials and biennials.

OCTOBER

OCTOBER, and autumn closes in on the garden. But it does so in a blaze of glory. Michaelmas daisies are at their most spectacular, a mixture of strong and pastel hues contributing vibrancy and immediacy to late season borders. They are not alone. This is a month for autumn bulbs – colchicums, crocus and cyclamen all commence their flowering season.

Spend time this month on some routine chores. Lawns will benefit from scarification where they have become compacted and should, in any case, be given an autumn feed. Continue to cut grass, with the mower blades set high. Winter digging may be started and any autumn pruning undertaken.

As this shows, the autumn garden need never be dull. Asters combine with late flowering perennials such as *Solidago* (golden rod) and sedums to produce an effective display. Note how the grass path is curved. This draws the eye on, suggesting something new just around the corner.

Reds and golds typify autumn so this strong combination of rudbeckia and physalis is totally in keeping. *Physalis alkekengii*, or Chinese lantern, produces these ornamental and edible fruits from inconspicuous cream flowers. 45 × 60cm/1½ × 2ft

This large stand of solidago contrasts well with a pale lilac Michaelmas daisy. Golden rod is inclined to be a spreading perennial. Short, compact varieties are available like *S. canadensis* 'Golden Baby' which grows to around 60cm/2ft.

Low-growing asters edge the path in this mixed border where the emphasis is firmly placed on providing a contrast of form and texture. Soft perennials serve to highlight the shapes of shrubs and evergreen trees.

Nerine bowdenii These bulbs prefer a warm situation in free-draining soil. ○, 45 × 20cm/1½ft × 8in

Autumn crocuses are suitable for an open, sunny position where they may be left to increase.

Liriope muscari Flowers are quite small and are often disguised by the leaves. 30 × 45cm/ 1 × 1½ft

Persicaria campanulata
An easy, spreading
perennial. 1 × 1m/
3 × 3ft

Colchicum speciosum
Sturdy flowers look
splendid in grass. ○,
20 × 20cm/8 × 8in

Cyclamen hederifolium
Flowers appear just as
the ivy-type leaves
begin to unfurl.
10 × 20cm/4 × 8in

***Physostegia virginiana* 'Variegata'** Leaves are
edged white which, combined with the dark lilac-
pink tubular flowers, make this a showy late
perennial. 30 × 30cm/1 × 1ft

SHRUBS AND TREES

Brilliant orange, burnished gold, crimson and bronze. The turning leaves of autumn are one of the principal joys of the season. Illustrated are the upright-growing *Malus tschonoskii*, the aptly named bonfire tree, *Acer palmatum* 'Osakazuki' and *Amelanchier* 'Ballerina'. All these are set against a background of the soft yellow leaves of *Rosa rugosa* 'Alba'.

Parthenocissus quinquefolia This is the true Virginia creeper which turns such an outstanding colour. A rampant self-clinging climber. 12m/39ft

Euonymus alatus Grow this bushy shrub for its autumn colour. 3 × 3m/ 10 × 10ft

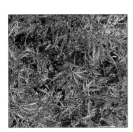

***Acer palmatum* 'Dissectum'** This compact acer is an excellent choice for a small garden where, growing slowly in part shade, it will eventually reach 1.2 × 1.5m/ 4 × 5ft.

Acer palmatum atropurpureum (*right*) Purple foliage becomes bright red at this time of year. 4.5 × 4.5m/ 15 × 15ft

Cotinus coggygria
'Royal Purple' Red
foliage after July
plumes. 4×4m/13×13ft

Vitis coignetiae The
crimson glory vine is
shown here trained on
a pillar. 15m/49ft

Liquidambar styraciflua Outstanding autumn
colouring. These leaves of richest claret will
remain on the tree well into winter. 16 × 8m/
52 × 26ft

Rhus glabra **'Laciniata'**
A very hardy, free-
suckering shrub which
is grown principally for
its late colour. Because
of its running habit it
can become a bit of a
nuisance. 3 × 3m/
10 × 10ft

This cottage wall is positively aglow with the bright berries of a wall trained pyracantha. E, 2.1m/7ft

◆ *Named forms include 'Dart's Red', 'Mohave' and 'Orange Charmer'.*

***Vitis vinifera*
'Purpurea'** Blue-black
grapes and leaves of
deep purple. 7m/23ft

Callicarpa bodinieri var.
geraldii Remarkable
berries. 4 × 4m/
13 × 13ft

Pernettya (syn.
Gaultheria) ***mucronata***
For acidic soil. ◐, E,
75cm × 1.2m/2½ × 4ft

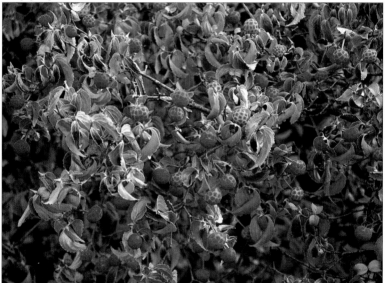

Cornus kousa Every garden should, if possible, contain a specimen of this
very elegant shrub. Summer flowers are followed by these fabulous,
decorative strawberry-like fruits. 3.6 × 4m/12 × 13ft

***Malus* 'Everest'** Dwarf tree with scarlet crab apples. 3.6 × 2.4m/ 12 × 8ft

Arbutus unedo Flowers and fruit appear together in the autumn. E, 5 × 5m/16 × 16ft

Rosa rugosa One of the pleasures of this rose is the bright red heps. ○, 1.5 × 1.5m/5 × 5ft

***Cotoneaster frigidus* 'Cornubia'** Clusters of scarlet berries hang in profusion below semi-evergreen leaves on this large tree-like shrub. Most types of cotoneaster reward with either foliage effects or massed berries. 7 × 7m/ 23 × 23ft

PLANT NEW HEDGES

October represents a good month in which to establish new hedges.

Ground must be well prepared in advance, incorporating where possible plenteous amounts of organic matter.

These new box plants will respond to an application of bonemeal in the spring to speed growth.

PLANT BARE-ROOTED ROSES

Specialist rose growers, and some garden centres, offer bare-rooted roses for sale throughout the autumn. Buying in this way makes good sense, not least because they are often considerably cheaper than those which are container grown.

Before planting, prune roses to shape, cutting above an outward facing bud. Also trim roots to encourage new growth.

CHECK LIST

◆ Scarify lawns and apply an autumn fertilizer (p.200).
◆ Start winter digging.
◆ Take account of autumn colour when choosing shrubs and trees (p.204).
◆ Plant bare-rooted roses (p.210).
◆ Establish new hedges (p.210).
◆ Begin preparations for winter (p.211).
◆ Plant tulips.

PUTTING THE GARDEN TO BED

Pots of tender plants need to be removed to a frost-free environment. Those which are to remain outside may need to be lagged as a precaution against damage or frost.

Cut down spent perennials, remove frosted annuals, lightly fork borders and apply a mulch if desired. Fallen leaves will start to pose problems in many cases. Sweep from lawns, remove from gulleys and clear from small plants.

LIFT TENDER PERENNIALS

Tender perennials should now be lifted. Dahlia tubers should be overwintered as described on page 184.

NOVEMBER

EVER SHORTENING DAYS, wet and windy weather, trees shedding their leaves, all make their mark on November. Increasingly interest depends on evergreen shrubs. Structure, in the form of bare trees, hedges and shapely plants begins to take over.

A carefully planned late autumn show. Seen against a background of dark leafed mahonia and golden variegated euonymus, the purple spikes of *Liriope platyphylla* are displayed to advantage.

Salix alba vitellina **'Britzensis'** The stems of this shrubby willow glow scarlet and orange in the late sun.

Brilliant red stems of *Cornus alba* are a handsome backdrop to a late yucca, in full flower.

Deep red, purple and white fruits of evergreen pernettya add sparkle to this artfully contrived composition.

For sheer elegance at the year's end there is little to rival the glorious plumes of the pampas grass, *Cortaderia selloana*.

***Viburnum tinus* 'Eve Price'** Flowering from now onwards. E, 2.4 × 2.4/8 × 8ft

***Viburnum* × *bodnantense* 'Dawn'** Beautifully scented shrub. 3.5 × 3.5m/12 × 12ft

Choisya ternata The Mexican orange blossom is hardy. E, 2 × 2m/6 × 6ft

Fatsia japonica Fatsia has the appearance of only being suitable for indoor cultivation. Tolerates sun or shade. E, 3 × 3m/10 × 10ft

Mahonia lomariifolia Sadly this magnificent scented mahonia is not fully hardy. E, 3 × 2m/10 × 6ft

Skimmia japonica Rich, seasonal berries come close to smothering this unfussy, evergreen shrub over the winter period. Grow skimmia to brighten up any dull or dark day. E, 60 × 60cm/2 × 2ft

Euonymus fortunei **'Emerald 'n' Gold'** The virtue of a shrub such as this one is that it has something to contribute all year. During autumn and winter its brightness is warmly appreciated. E, 1 × 1.5m/3 × 5ft

***Elaeagnus pungens* 'Dicksonii'** An ideal shrub with which to brighten up a featureless border. As with all variegated shrubs care should be taken to cut out any branches where the leaves have reverted. ○, E, 2.4 × 3m/8 × 10ft

Hedera colchica **'Sulphur Heart'** Long, rather drooping leaves are lifted with
bold splashes of yellow on this evergreen climbing ivy. Ivies thrive in almost
any situation and are very tolerant of atmospheric pollution. E, 4.5m/15ft

Aucuba japonica **'Gold
Dust'** All the aucubas
are valuable shrubs for
difficult situations. The
leaves of this particular
form are speckled gold.
Red berries are
produced from autumn
to spring. E, 2.4 × 2.4m/
8 × 8ft

Many hollies are suitable
for training against walls
or for clipping into a
variety of shapes. *Ilex
aquifolium* 'J.C. van Tol' is
used here to clothe the
wall of a house. This
particular holly has
virtually spineless leaves
and produces a good crop
of red berries.

***Cornus stolonifera*
'Flaviramea'** Grow for
its yellow stems.
2 × 4m/6 × 12ft

***Lonicera nitida*
'Baggesen's Gold'** may
be clipped into shape.
○, E, 1.5 × 2m/5 × 6ft

***Thuja occidentalis* 'Rheingold'** Conifers come into
their own during winter. E, 3 × 1.5m/10 × 5ft

***Ligustrum ovalifolium* 'Aureum'** Golden privet is a
useful, fast-growing shrub. Semi-evergreen, it will
lose its leaves if the winter is severe. 4 × 3m/
13 × 10ft

***Vinca minor*
'Aureovariegata'**
Ground cover plant. E,
15cm/6in (spread
indefinite)

GARDEN WASTE
Leaves swept from lawns will make excellent leaf mould.

With the exception of woody stems, which should be chopped, shredded or burnt, all garden and household waste should be composted. Left to rot for eighteen months or so it will make an excellent medium with which to enrich the soil.

ATTEND TO GARDEN PONDS
Where possible, clear debris from the water.

Cut down surrounding perennials and fork over the soil. Giant leaves of *Gunnera manicata* should be folded over the crown of the plant to provide protection from cold.

Submersible pumps may be removed, serviced and stored in preparation for next season.

Finally, fish will survive the winter months without feeding.

DIG AND MANURE VEGETABLE BEDS
Over winter prepare for spring by digging and manuring the kitchen garden.

TAKE HARDWOOD CUTTINGS

Many trees and shrubs, like this *Sambucus* (elder), are readily propagated from hardwood cuttings.

Select a cutting 30cm/1ft in length. Cut at the top just above a leaf joint and at the bottom below a joint. Dip the lower part into a hormone rooting powder.

Dig a small trench in a shady spot and rest the bottom of the labelled cutting on to this base. Infill with soil.

Cuttings should root within twelve months.

CHECK LIST

◆ Choose variegated and evergreen shrubs for year-round interest (pp.214–219).
◆ Clear ponds of autumn debris, service electrical pumps and stop feeding fish (p.220).
◆ Collect leaves for leaf mould (p.220).
◆ Manure vegetable beds (p.220).
◆ Take hardwood cuttings (p.221).
◆ Plant bare-rooted trees and shrubs (p.27).
◆ Complete the planting of tulips as soon as possible this month.

PLANT FRUIT TREES
Late autumn is the time to plant fruit trees. Prepare ground beforehand and stake where necessary.

DECEMBER

WITH DECEMBER, and the approach of winter, the garden takes on an air of quietness.

Cold but clear wintery days may be used to tackle those jobs which are forgotten during busier times. Trees and shrubs which overhang or obstruct paths may be pruned back to give ease of access. Ditches, gulleys and drains cleaned out and kept clear will prevent a build-up of surface water during periods of heavy rainfall. Apply wood preservative to garden seats and sheds and structures such as pergolas, archways and trellises.

Look carefully and critically at the hard landscaping and structure of the garden, noting how it may be improved in the coming year.

Frosted heads of *Stipa gigantea*, a large clump-forming grass, make a dramatic impact seen against the woolly, grey-green foliage of *Ozothamnus rosmarinifolius*.

***Miscanthus sinensis* 'Silver Feather'**
Grasses are an excellent foil to other
plantings. 2m × 60cm/6 × 2ft

Fargesia nitida This small leafed
bamboo is noted for its distinctive
purplish stems. E, 5m/15ft ×
indefinite spread

The approach to this
cottage is
sympathetically planted
with a series of clipped
yew cones. In winter,
possibly in snow, their
structure would be even
more pronounced.

Picea glauca **'Albertiana'** for rock gardens. E, 1m × 45cm/ 3 × 1½ft

Abies balsamea f. *hudsonia* slow-growing form of the Balsam fir. E, 1 × 1m/3 × 3ft

Juniperus communis **'Compressa'** A tiny evergreen tree. E, 75 × 15cm/2½ft × 6in

Juniperus horizontalis **'Wiltonii'** Permanent ground cover is achieved by planting this low, spreading juniper of steely-blue. The ultimate spread is likely to be around 4m/13ft.

Hebe **'Boughton Dome'**
Fine foliage makes up
for the few flowers. E,
75×75cm/$2\frac{1}{2} \times 2\frac{1}{2}$ft

Brachyglottis **'Sunshine'**
Evergreen grey foliage
is valuable in winter. ○,
E, 1.2×2m/4×6ft

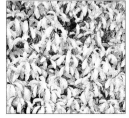

Pittosporum tenuifolium
Highly ornamental,
evergreen shrubs. E,
5×4m/16×13ft

Beautifully grown box spirals flank the approach
to this flight of steps. A small leafed ivy softens the
elegant, basket-weave containers.

Jasminum nudiflorum Winter jasmine is much loved and, accordingly, widely grown. Here it has been trained to smother a wall with its splendid yellow blossom and green, whippy stems. 3m/10ft

Iris foetidissima Seed pods of the Gladwin iris burst open in winter. E, 45 × 60cm/1½ × 2ft

Arum italicum Winter sees the emergence of these wonderful leaves. ●, 25 × 20cm/10 × 8in

Euphorbia myrsinites Heavy frost on this ground-hugging euphorbia. ○, E, 15 × 60cm/6in × 2ft

Garrya elliptica Favour this handsome shrub with a warm wall to afford it protection from the worst of the frosts. Long-lasting male catkins may open as early as November or, depending on the weather, be delayed until February. E, 4 × 3m/13 × 10ft

COLD WEATHER PRECAUTIONS

A little time spent affording some of the plants in the garden protection from the worst of the weather will pay dividends.

Unwanted conifer branches are used here to blanket a tender climber. Perennials of doubtful hardiness will usually come through if the crown is covered either with a mulch of compost or old fern leaves weighted down. Garden fleece is useful for protecting tender plants.

Wind will also be a problem. Check ties and stakes on all vulnerable shrubs. Cut back a third of each stem of tree mallows (*Lavatera*) to prevent wind rock. If you prune roses in autumn instead of spring (see page 38) you will lessen the danger of wind rock, but new shoots might suffer frost damage.

CHECK LIST

- Prune overhanging trees and shrubs (p.222).
- Clean out ditches and drains (p.222).
- Apply preservative to exposed wood (p.222).
- Give tender plants some form of protection (p.228).
- Dislodge snow from trees and shrubs (p.228).
- Protect plants from wind (p.228).
- Switch off outside water (p.228).
- Care for wildlife (p.229).

CARING FOR WILDLIFE
At times when the temperature consistently remains below freezing, melt a small area of ice on the pond to release trapped gases that could be harmful to fish. This may be gently done by holding a container of boiling water on the surface.

Birds will be grateful for any scraps put out for them.

STORE TERRACOTTA POTS
Terracotta pots are not necessarily frost resistant. Hessian secured around pots will prevent the clay from splintering.

Anemone blanda 'White Splendour'

CALENDAR

The following are chronological flowering lists, though in some cases shrubs have been included for their interesting foliage or fruits. The precise month of flowering will often vary according to weather and location; for this reason the season has been given after each month and it may be helpful to use this when planning planting schemes. Flowering periods will in any case overlap calendar months and many plants will remain in flower for several weeks or even months.

Numbers in brackets refer to pages where plants are described.

January–February (Early Year)

Chionodoxa (Glory of the snow) (17)
Crocus (14, 17)
Cyclamen coum (15)
Eranthis (Winter aconite) (16)
Galanthus (Snowdrop) (16)
Hellebores (16)
Hepatica

Iris danfordiae
  I. histrioides
  I. reticulata (17)
  I. unguicularis (Algerian iris) (14)
Narcissus bulbocodium (Hoop-petticoat
  daffodil) (17)

Lysichiton americanus

N. cyclamineus
Pulmonaria (Lungwort) (34)
Scilla mischtschenkoana

SHRUBS AND TREES
Abeliophyllum distichum
Chimonathus praecox (Wintersweet) (22)
Clematis cirrhosa (22)
Cornus mas
Daphne odora (23)
Erica carnea (Heather) (23)
  E. darleyensis
Garrya elliptica (Tassel bush) (227)
Hamamelis (Witch hazel) (21)
Jasminum nudiflorum (Winter jasmine) (226)
Lonicera fragrantissima (23)
Prunus × subhirtella 'Autumnalis'
Sarcococca (Sweet box) (21)
Viburnum tinus (214)

March (Early Spring)

Anemone appenina (33)
  A. blanda
Bergenia (34)
Corydalis (32)
Crocus (17)
Darmera peltata (Umbrella plant)
Doronicum (Leopard's bane) (46)
Epimedium (Barrenwort) (32)
Erythronium dens-canis (Dog's-tooth violet) (35)
Hellebore (34)
Iberis
Ipheion (33)
Lysichiton americanus (Yellow skunk cabbage)
Muscari (Grape hyacinth) (29)
Narcissus hybrids (Daffodils) (29)
Omphalodes cappadocica

231

Darmera peltata

Primula (Primrose, Polyanthus) (31, 32, 44, 45)
Pulmonaria (Lungwort) (34)
Ranunculus (Buttercup) (34)
Scilla (31)
Symphytum grandiflorum (Comfrey)
Tulipa greigii
  T. kaufmanniana (28)
Viola odorata (Sweet violet)

SHRUBS & TREES
Camellia (36)
Corylopsis pauciflora
Daphne mezereum
  D. blagayana
Erica arborea (Tree heath)
Forsythia (36)
Mahonia aquifolium
Parrotia
Pieris (23)

Prunus dulcis (Ornamental almond)
  P. mume (Japanese apricot)
  P. × yedoensis (Yoshino cherry)
Rhododendron 'Praecox' (36)
Sycopsis sinensis
Viburnum × burkwoodii (36)

April (Spring)

Alyssum saxatile (50)
Anemone nemorosa (51)
Arabis (48)
Arum (Cuckoo pint) (45)
Aubrieta (49)
Bellis (Daisy) (66)
Brunnera (46)
Caltha palustris (Marsh marigold) (47)
Cheiranthus (Wallflower) (41)
Cortusa matthioli
Dicentra (47, 51)

Dodecatheon meadia

Dodecatheon meadia
Doronicum (Leopard's bane) (46)
Euphorbia (Spurge) (50)
Fritillaria (Fritillary) (42, 43)
Hyacinth (40)
Lamium (Deadnettle) (44)
Leucojum vernum (Spring snowflake) (42)
Lunaria (Honesty) (64, 65)
Lysichiton camschatcensis (Skunk cabbage) (47)
Muscari (Grape hyacinth)
Narcissus (Daffodil) (42)
Ornithogalum nutans (Star of Bethlehem)
Oxalis acetosella (Wood sorrel)
Polygonatum (Solomon's seal)
Primula (44, 45)
Pulsatilla vulgaris (Pasque flower) (49)
Sanguinaria canadensis (50)
Saxifrage (51)
Silene dioica (Red campion)

Symphytum grandiflorum (Comfrey)
Tulips, early hybrids (41, 48)
Uvularia grandiflora (Bellwort) (46)
Veronica 'Georgia Blue' (45)
Vinca (Periwinkle)
Viola (Pansy)

SHRUBS & TREES
Acer pseudoplatanus 'Brilliantissimum' (53)
Amelanchier
Berberis (Barberry) (56)
Camellia (54)
Ceanothus impressus
Chaenomeles (53)
Choisya (79)
Clematis (57)
Coronilla glauca
Cytisus (79)
Daphne × *burkwoodii*
Fothergilla

Geranium malviflorum

Kerria
Magnolia (54)
Malus (Crab apple) (56)
Osmanthus (56)
Prunus (Japanese cherry tree) (55)
Pyrus salicifolia 'Pendula'
Rhododendron hybrids (55)
Ribes (Currant)
Salix (Willow) (52, 56)
Skimmia (56)
Spiraea 'Arguta' (Bridal wreath) (79)
Viburnum × burkwoodii
  V. × juddii (55)

May (Late Spring/Early Summer)

Ajuga (Bugle)
Allium aflatunense (74)
Anthemis punctata (Chamomile)
Aquilegia (Columbine) (62)

Arisaema
Armeria (Thrift) (64)
Asphodeline lutea (110)
Camassia (75)
Cardamine pratensis (Lady's smock)
Celmisia
Centaurea (66)
Convallaria (Lily-of-the-valley) (75)
Dicentra (69)
Disporum sessile
Erinus alpinus (Fairy foxglove)
Erodium
Euphorbia (Spurge) (65)
Gentiana acaulis (67)
Geranium (Cranesbill) e.g. *G. malviflorum*
Geum rivale (70)
Helianthemum (103, 104)
Hesperis (Sweet rocket) (69)
Hyacinthoides non-scriptus (Bluebell) (74)
Incarvillea delavayi

Rheum palmatum

Iris, Californian hybrids (71)
Jeffersonia diphylla
Lavandula stoechas (Lavender) (122)
Leucojum aestivum (Summer snowflake)
Libertia (67)
Limnanthes (Poached egg flower) (70)
Linum
Lithodora diffusa
Lunaria (Honesty) (64, 65)
Meconopsis cambrica (Welsh poppy) (64)
Mertensia (70)
Myosotis (Forget-me-not) (64, 73)
Narcissus 'Hawera'
  N. poeticus var. *recurvus* (Pheasant's eye)
Orontium aquaticum (89)
Paeonia arietina (71)
  P. mlokosewitschii
  P. tenuifolia
Parochetus communis
Penstemon ('rock garden' forms)

Persicaria bistorta (Bistort)
Phlox (64)
Polemonium (107)
Primula sieboldii (68)
Rheum palmatum
Rhodohypoxis (74)
Smilacina (68)
Tellima grandiflora
Thalictrum (62)
Thermopsis (70)
Tiarella cordifolia (Foamflower)
Tolmiea menziesii
Trillium (68)
Trollius
Tulips (72, 73)
Vancouveria hexandra
Veronica gentianoides (67)
Viola (64, 67)

Daphne × burkwoodii

SHRUBS & TREES
Abutilon (125, 129)
Aesculus (76)
Akebia quinata (Chocolate vine)
Andromeda
Azaleas (84, 85)
Berberis thunbergii
Ceanothus (82)
Cercis (Judas tree) (78)
Choisya ternata (79)
Clematis montana (81) and early large
    flowered clematis
Convolvulus cneorum (83)
Crataegus (Hawthorn)
Crinodendron hookeranum
Cytisus (79)
Daphne × burkwoodii
    D. tangutica
Drimys winteri
Eccremocarpus scaber (Chilean glory vine)

Embothrium coccineum
Exochorda (79)
Fothergilla (87)
Fremontodendron (87)
Genista (Broom) (87)
Halesia (Snowdrop tree) (83)
Hebe pinguifolia
Laburnum (87)
Leptospermum
Leucothoë
Lithodora
Magnolia liliiflora
Malus (Crab apple) (76)
Paeonia delavayi (Tree peony) (83)
    P. suffruticosa (Tree peony) (83)
Paulownia
Pernettya
Philadelphus coronarius (Mock orange) (125)
Piptanthus
Potentilla (145)

Viburnum plicatum 'Mariesii'

Prunus – Japanese cherries (78)
Rhododendron (84, 85)
Rosa banksiae and early yellow roses (86)
  R. moyesii (86)
  R. rugosa (86)
Rubus tridel
Solanum crispum (121)
Sorbus aria (Whitebeam) (77)
Spiraea (79)
Syringa (Lilac) (80)
Tamarix gallica (Tamarisk)
Viburnum davidii
  V. opulus (Guelder rose)
  V. plicatum 'Mariesii'
Weigela (80)
Wisteria (88)

June (Early Summer/Midsummer)

Aethionema
Alchemilla (101)
Allium christophii
  A. moly
Alstroemeria (136)
Anchusa
Anthericum
Aruncus
Asarina procumbens
Asphodeline (Asphodel) (110)
Asphodelus (Asphodel) (106)
Astrantia (Masterwort)
Baptisia (106)
Campanula (Bellflower) e.g. *C. latiloba*
Centaurea macrocephala (110)
Centranthus (Valerian) (103)
Cephalaria (110)
Corydalis lutea (102)
Crambe cordifolia (109)
Dactylorrhiza (Orchid)
Delphinium (111)

Dictamnus albus 'Purpureus'

Dianthus (Pink) (102)
Dictamnus (Burning bush)
Digitalis (Foxglove) (99)
Eremurus (Foxtail lily)
Erigeron (Fleabane)
Geranium (Cranesbill) e.g. *G. endressii* (98)
Geum (70)
Gillenia (108)
Gladiolus byzantinus (99)
Helianthemum (104)
Hemerocallis (63, 149, 166)
Heuchera (193)
Hosta (111)
Iris (100, 107)
Kniphofia (Red-hot poker) e.g. *K. 'Atlanta'*
Lathyrus grandiflorus (Everlasting pea)
Lilium martagon (Martagon lily) (108)
Linum
Lupinus arboreus (Tree lupin) (128)
  L. polyphyllus (Lupin) (101)

Lychnis (74, 105)
Lysimachia punctata (137)
Mitella breweri
Nepeta (Catmint) (99)
Nicotiana (152)
Nigella damascena (Love-in-a-mist)
Nuphar lutea (Yellow water lily)
Nymphaea (Water lily)
Osteospermum (136)
Paeonia (Peony) (104)
Papaver orientale (Oriental poppy) (104)
Penstemon (104)
Phuopsis stylosa
Polemonium (107)
Primula vialii (167)
Ruta graveolens (Rue)
Salvia (107)
Scabiosa (Scabious) (100)
Sisyrinchium striatum
Stachys macrantha (106)

Erigeron karvinskianus

Stipa (222)
Thalictrum aquilegifolium (62)
Thermopsis (70)
Verbascum
Veronica 'Shirley Blue' (142)
Viola cornuta (108, 109)

SHRUBS & TREES
Abutilon (125, 129)
Brachyglottis (syn. *Senecio*) (128)
Buddleja alternifolia (129)
  B. globosa (128)
Bupleurum
Carpenteria (129)
Cistus, e.g. × *hybridus* (122)
Clematis, mid-season large-flowered, e.g.
  'Mrs. Cholmondeley' (129)
Colutea arborescens
Cornus canadensis
  C. kousa (124)

  C. nuttallii
Davidia
Deutzia (127)
Embothrium
Enkianthus
Fabiana
Fremontodendron (87)
× *Halimiocistus* (122)
Hebe macrantha
Hydrangea anomala subsp. *petiolare* (124)
Kalmia (Calico bush) (128)
Kolkwitzia (Beauty bush) (129)
Laburnum (87)
Lavandula (Lavender) (122)
Lavatera 'Barnsley' (127)
Lonicera (Honeysuckle) (127)
Magnolia, e.g. M. × *watsonii* (127)
Neillia (126)
Philadelphus (Mock orange), e.g. 'Belle
  Etoile' (125)

Cardiocrinum giganteum

Phlomis (128)
Potentilla fruticosa (145)
Rhododendron hybrids and late-flowering
  Azalea species
Roses, Old French, many shrub roses,
  climbers and ramblers
Schizandra
Solanum crispum (121)
Styrax

July (Midsummer)

Abutilon megapotamicum (144)
Acanthus (175)
Achillea (Yarrow) (147)
Agapanthus (140)
Agastache
Alstroemeria (136)
Amsonia (Blue star)
Anthemis tinctoria (137)

Arisaema
Aster × frikartii 'Mönch' (137)
Astilbe (164, 165)
Bedding Plants
  Many of these annuals and tender subjects
  will be in flower until the first frosts:
Ageratum (152)
Alyssum
Antirrhinum (153)
Argyranthemum (Marguerite) (154)
Begonia (93)
Calendula (Marigold) (174)
Chrysanthemum parthenium (153)
Iberis (Candytuft)
Impatiens (Busy Lizzie) (153)
Lantana
Lobelia (160, 161)
Nemesia
Nicotiana (152)
Pansy (161)

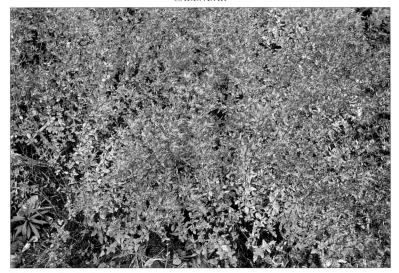

Origanum laevigatum

Pelargonium (160)
Petunia (174)
Salvia splendens (153)
Tagetes (Marigold) (96, 174)
Verbena
Calamintha
Campanula (Bellflower) e.g. *C. alliariifolia* (141)
Canna (146)
Cardiocrinum
Catananche
Cimicifuga racemosa
Codonopsis
Convolvulus sabatius (137)
Coreopsis verticillata
Delphinium (143)
Dictamnus
Epilobium (Bay willow herb) (135)
Erigeron
Eryngium (137, 141)

Eupatorium
Filipendula (Meadowsweet) (167)
Gillenia (108)
Gypsophila (190)
Helichrysum italicum (149)
Hemerocallis hybrids (166)
Hosta (111)
Hyssopus officinalis (Hyssop)
Iris, e.g. *I. laevigata*
Kniphofia (Red-hot poker), e.g. *K.* 'Little Maid' (149)
Lathyrus latifolius (Everlasting pea) (142)
Liatris spicata (172)
Ligularia przewalskii (166)
Lilium (Lily), e.g. *L. regale* (163)
Lysimachia punctata (137)
Lythrum salicaria (Purple loosestrife)
Malva moschata
Monarda (136)
Nepeta (Catmint) (99)

Tradescantia 'Purple Dome'

Oenothera (149)
Origanum
Osteospermum (136)
Penstemon e.g. *P.* 'Apple Blossom' (136)
Persicaria affinis (167)
Phlox (140)
Primula florindae (166)
  P. vialii (167)
Rodgersia (167)
Romneya
Salvia patens (142)
Sanguisorba
Selinum tenuifolium
Sidalcea
Stachys olympica
Strobilanthes
Tradescantia
Tropaeolum (145)
  T. majus (Nasturtium) (146)
Veratrum

Verbena bonariensis (135)
Veronica austriaca 'Shirley Blue' (142)
Zantedeschia aethiopica (166)

SHRUBS & TREES
Abelia
Buddleja globosa (128)
Callistemon rigidus (Bottlebrush) (145)
Calluna vulgaris
Catalpa
Ceratostigma
Clematis × *durandii* (149)
  C. viticella varieties (183, 195)
Cytisus battandieri (Morrocan broom) (159)
Escallonia (159)
Fuchsia (154)
Genista aetnensis (Mount Etna broom) (159)
Hebe hybrids (158)
Hoheria
Hydrangea arborescens

Passiflora 'Constance Elliot'

Hypericum calycinum (Rose of Sharon) (145)
Indigofera (158)
Lavandula (Lavender) (158)
Lavatera maritima (158)
Lonicera (Honeysuckle), e.g. *L. tragophylla* (151)
Maackia amurensis
Melianthus major (Honeybush)
Passiflora (Passion flower)
Phygelius
Potentilla (145)
Rosa – Floribunda (Cluster-flowered) varieties
  R. filipes (156)
  Hybrid Tea varieties
Santolina (Cotton lavender)
Solanum jasminoides (142)
Sorbaria (159)
Spartium
Spiraea

August (Late Summer)

Adenophora (Gland bellflower)
Alcea rosea (Hollyhock) (171)
Anemone hupehensis (Japanese anemone) (188)
  A. × *hybrida* (Japanese anemone) (188)
Aster thompsonii 'Nanus' (189)
Buphthalmum
Canna (146)
Clematis heracleifolia (175)
Crinum
Crocosmia (171)
Curtonus
Echinacea (187)
Echinops (175)
Gentiana asclepiadea
Helenium (171)
Helianthus (171, 190)
Knautia

Fuchsia 'Lena' and *Clematis jackmanii* 'Superba'

Kniphofia, e.g. *K.* 'Cobra'
Lilium, e.g. Oriental lilies
Limonium
Lobelia cardinalis (172)
Macleaya
Sedum 'Ruby Glow' (175)
Senecio tanguticus (190)
Tritonia

SHRUBS & TREES

Aralia elata (181)
Buddleja davidii (182)
Campsis
Caryopteris (180)
Ceanothus × *delileanus* 'Gloire de Versailles' (181)
Clematis viticella and late large-flowered forms (183)
Dorycnium
Escallonia 'Iveyi' (159)

Eucryphia (178)
Eupatorium
Fuchsia (172)
Hibiscus (181)
Hydrangeas (179)
Itea (180)
Koelreuteria (178)
Magnolia grandiflora (181)
Perovskia (180)
Polygonum baldschuanicum (183)
Potentilla fruticosa (145)
Schizophragma (183)
Tamarix ramosissima (Tamarisk) (176)
Yucca gloriosa (180)

September (Early Autumn)

Aconitum carmichaelii (189)
Arctotis (190)
Asters (Michaelmas daisies) (189)

Dendranthema 'Julia'

Dendranthema (171)
Echinacea (Coneflower) (187)
Gypsophila (190)
Helianthus (Sunflower) (171, 190)
Kirengeshoma (190)
Kniphofia (189)
Lobelia (172)
Miscanthus (223)
Rudbeckia (191)
Schizostylis (Kaffir lily) (189)
Sedum (175)

SHRUBS & TREES
Buddleja crispa (193)
Clematis tangutica and late-flowering species
 (195–6)
Clerodendrum (193)
Leycesteria (192)
Parthenocissus (leaf colour) (197, 205)

October (Autumn)

Autumn crocus (202)
Colchicum (203)
Cyclamen hederifolium (203)
Liriope (202)
Nerine (202)
Persicaria (203)
Physalis (Chinese lantern) (201)
Physostegia (203)
Solidago (Golden rod) (201)
Tricyrtis (Toad lily)

SHRUBS & TREES
Arbutus unedo (Strawberry tree)
Autumn fruits
 Callicarpa (208)
 Cornus (Dogwood) 208
 Cotoneaster (209)
 Malus (Crab apple) (209)

Pyracantha

Pernettya (208)
Pyracantha (Firethorn) (207)
Roses (209)
Viburnum opulus (Guelder rose)
Autumn leaf colour
  Acer (Maple) (205)
  Amelanchier (204)
  Cotinus (Smoke bush) (206)
  Euonymus (205)
  Liquidamber (207)
  Parthenocissus (197, 205)
  Rhus (Sumach) (206)
  Vitis (Vine) (206, 208)

November (Late Autumn)

SHRUBS & TREES
Aucuba (217)
Choisya ternata (214)
Fatsia (214)

Hippophae rhamnoides
Mahonia lomariifolia (214)
Skimmia (215)
Viburnum × bodnantense (214)
  V. tinus (214)

December (Early Winter)

Iris unguicularis (Algerian iris) (14)

SHRUBS & TREES
Garrya elliptica (Tassel bush) (227)
Jasminum nudiflorum (Winter jasmine) (226)

INDEX

255